# The Art of
# Being Rational

# The Art of Being Rational

**CHARLIE MUNGER**

Oxana Dubrovina

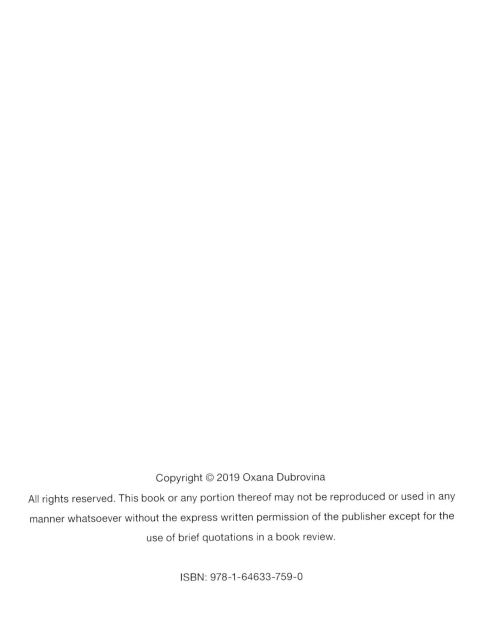

ISBN: 978-1-64633-759-0

"I am trying to emulate my great grandfather. When he died, they said about him, nobody envied the success so fairly won and wisely used. It is a simple philosophy. Wouldn't Wall Street have worked better if more people had tried to imitate my grandfather"[i]?

Charlie Munger, CNBC interview, Sunday, May 6, 2012

# Table of Contents

# Introduction. Why I Am Writing This Book

My story. First, let me tell you something about myself. I am Russian, but I was born in Samarkand, Uzbekistan, in the former Soviet Union. After the collapse of the Soviet Union, my family moved to Moscow, Russia. I graduated with a law degree from the Academy of Labor and Social Relation in Moscow. In 2005, I moved to Vienna, Austria, to pursue a law degree at the University of Vienna. Through the years, I worked for different big and local international law firms in Vienna.

Now I live and work in Vienna. The first question you may ask me is what does this have to do with Charlie Munger and Warren Buffett? Let me answer this question systematically. I would like to give you an example from psychology, as illustrated in a book by Robert Cialdini, *Influence: The Psychology of Persuasion*.[ii]

Cialdini starts by discussing the mothering instinct of turkeys. Mother turkeys are very protective, good mothers, but their mothering instinct has been found to be triggered by one thing and one thing only: the "cheep-cheep" sound of their chicks. The polecat is the natural enemy of the turkey, and when a mother turkey sees one, she will instantly go into attack mode; she will do so even at the sight of a stuffed version of a polecat. But when the same stuffed polecat is made to make the same "cheep-cheep" sound that her chicks make, something strange happens: the mother turkey becomes a devoted protector of it!

You may think: How dumb are animals? Press a button, and they act a certain way, even if those actions are ridiculous. But Cialdini tells us about turkey behavior only to prepare us for the uncomfortable truth about human automatic reaction. We also have our "preprogrammed tapes," which usually work for us in positive ways—for instance, to ensure our survival without having to think too much—but they can also be played to our detriment when we are unaware of the triggers.

The principle of the "cheep-cheep" sound illustrates the connection I have with my relatives or somebody whom I know very well. We are usually interested in a person who looks the same, who behaves the same, and everything we do goes together with psychology, which influences our decisions and thoughts in everyday matters. In my case, it is about my grandfather who reminds me of Charlie Munger. My grandfather died many years ago. I miss the old-school values of moral and ethics that my grandfather represented. Charlie represents a high intellect with the continuation of these high standards of morals and ethics. I believe that Charlie Munger is a most rational person, while Warren Buffett is a genius in his own way. They have a lot in common, despite being different characters, but represent the same values and principles.

In one CNBC interview, after they discussed how Warren Buffett wants to be remembered as a teacher, Charlie said: "Well I have a little different twist. I have less ambition than Warren of being a great teacher. I am trying to emulate my great grandfather. When he died they said about him, nobody envied the success so fairly won and wisely used. It is a simple philosophy. Wouldn't Wall Street have worked better if more people had tried to imitate my grandfather?"[iii]

This book is not a typical Value Investing Book; it is not the aim to teach you how to get rich easy or recommend stocks you should buy. This book is a collection of thoughts put together on morals and ethics and the life of Charlie Munger as a novel. I tried to put his quotes and his thoughts on different matters together in Part 1 as a story. I combined small puzzles to make it much more fun for the reader, to help you understand it better. I believe when you have his quotes presented in a story, it will help make it easier to understand; his writing and speeches are in their pure form.

You may ask, if my interest is Charlie Munger, why I am writing on both Charlie Munger and Warren Buffett. Well, first I started to focus on Charlie exclusively but later understood it is impossible to separate them. Both men are very connected; they have influenced each other's decisions throughout the years. Exactly this cooperation of two minds made Berkshire Hathaway one of the best financial conglomerates ever created based on two great intellects, Charlie Munger and Warren Buffett. As I started to be interested in Charlie Munger in 2014, I made a fan group on Facebook, "Charlie Munger Almanack." After a while, I concluded that if I did not put his beautiful ideas and facts in a book, they would be wasted and lost with time. You should approach this book with an open mind and adopt the best ideas and lessons as you see fit, or maybe you will even change your mind on certain subjects after reading this book. I hope this book will influence many people's minds, especially young people, helping them to be more rational and objective.

"Nobody is that clever to sit and dream it himself,"[iv] Charlie Munger said.

As Darwin said: "When I have found out that I have blundered or that my work has been imperfect, and when I have been overpraised, so that I have felt mortified, it has been my greatest comfort to say hundreds of times to myself 'I have worked as hard as well I could, and no man can do more than this.' I remember when in Good Success Bay in Tierre del Fuego thinking (and, believe, that I wrote home to the effect) that I could not employ my life better than in adding a little to national science. This I have done to the best of my abilities, and critics may say what they like but they cannot destroy this conviction."[v]

This point of view of Darwin reflects exactly what I want to tell you. I have worked on this book to make it interesting and amusing so every reader will find the content useful.

Why do I concentrate your attention on morals and ethics, faults and mistakes? Well, it comes back to my personal story. I was raised in a family with "two fathers," my own father and my grandfather. Each of them had a strong influence on me. I spent a lot of time with my grandfather in my childhood. He was very kind, a very special person. Of course, you may have great ethics and moral principles in your family but never take it to your business. But why don't we put the right principles and values in our everyday business life as well?

As Charlie articulated: "Nothing is more important than behaving well in life."[vi]

We do lack great people in a leadership in business right now. The last generations of struggle in Russia made a business society that is moved and ruled by the principles of an ecosystem, so the strongest are going to survive without any attention to humanity and ethics; if you speak about using honestly and moral in business, they think it is maybe a joke or you are a very naive and weak person. After the collapse of the Soviet Union, the former USSR republics were economically poor due to the lack of an intelligent, effective systematic approach in business, of well-educated people, of wisdom, of respectable people in both business and social life. Of course, the international characteristics of modern businesses are far from excellent. It is difficult to find a good model of behavior to learn from in the modern world, to copy their ideas. Maybe they are all already gone, so you could learn it from the past. Therefore, I focused my attention on Charlie Munger and Warren Buffett—exceptional people offering an intelligent, honest, and moral approach to business and life.

If you believe I have written this book to make you rich fast, please put it down, as this book is not about making money. I will not give you advice on picking stocks. I personally have nothing to do with stocks, but in capital allocation, it is an unavoidable subject to think about. You need to invest in your lifetime, so you must read and learn to educate yourself, like it or not.

Ignoring the subject of further education and everyday learning is unwise. "It is dishonorable to be stupider than you have to be."[vii] After all my Charlie Munger reading and research, I could not agree more with Bill Gates, who said, "Charlie Munger is the broadest thinker I have ever seen."

I personally think Charlie has been highly underestimated under Berkshire Hathaway's and Warren Buffett's influence. Charlie Munger is a pure reincarnation of Benjamin Franklin: great ideas on self-education, high ethical standards, and a multidisciplinary approach. Could you imagine Benjamin Franklin as a person, his great mind "being closed" in one company like Berkshire Hathaway, as an example? This is what has happened with Charlie. Of course, now it is one of the best companies in the world, ruling on principles of honesty, lifetime learning, discipline, and rationalism.

Charlie Munger character and personality—he is mostly a quiet and silent partner on Buffett's side as advisor and friend—turns out to be great for him. Charlie does not like direct interaction with the public like Warren Buffett. Charlie is too direct and does not suffer fools at all. Therefore, his direct approach makes him many enemies.

Charlie is a very useful partner for Warren. Charlie cuts right to the heart of any issue or problem. He served as "truth teller or filter"[viii] in many situations, as exemplified in the Solomon crisis. Everybody needs intelligent and honest partners to make then work well, but I want you to draw your own conclusions. I am a writer only, so my opinion could be too subjective, so make up your own mind. My role is to give you as much information as I can.

I am happy and lucky to have my husband to help me on editing this book, make correction and support my ideas for this project. I also want to apologies for possible mistakes you may find in this book.

Sincerely,
Oxana

# The Art of Being Rational: Charlie Munger

Charlie Munger is a modern-day philosopher, investor, philanthropist, and ideal family father of our time, but of course, he is famous for his partnership with Warren Buffett.

His children called him a "book with two legs sticking outside." I will call him the most rational person in the world. Charlie: "Rationality is not something you do so that you can make more money; it is binding principle. Rationality is a really good idea. You must avoid the nonsense that is conventional in one's own time. It requires developing a system of thought that improves your betting average over time[ix]."

An independent thinker who hates the crowd opinion. His direct and honest approach in business and life has created for him a big fan club. Thousands of Charlie Munger's and Warren Buffett's fans visit every Berkshire Hathaway annual meeting. At the Daily Journal Corporation meeting, where Charlie is chairman, he told a crowd of people in the room: "You are not ordinary shareholders. You are all investment groupies which are heavily addicted to a certain attitude of life[x]." I highly admire Charlie personality, his ethical and moral standards. His intellect and worldly wisdom could have an enormous influence on the education of the modern generation.

Charlie and Warren acquired and accumulated their wisdom through continuous learning and reading different kinds of literature. To get the best results in the world, you have to follow the rule of learning. Berkshire Hathaway is the most successful financial conglomerate on this planet. Because it has a great corporate culture, I am happy to write a book about it. Behave well as you go through life. Over time, you will get the reputation you deserve.

The Berkshire Hathaway annual meeting in 2017 brought forty thousand people together, waiting in a line from 5:00 a.m. You know the people who are in the line are already rich, so do you really believe they came there only because of money or because Berkshire earned a lot of money? To a certain extent, these people were looking for wisdom and sincerity. The answer is this combination of the great minds of Charlie Munger and Warren Buffet and their exceptional culture. Kind of hero's cultivation is not happening around the world—this is Berkshire Hathaway.

I personally do not believe this culture and principle will be forgotten with time, as they are timeless. Therefore, humans will stay the same: crazy greed, crazy leverage—you heard it yesterday; you will hear it tomorrow as well. Could this book give you a set of guiding principles? Yes, but you decide your own rules. Why do I consider this book different from other books about Charlie Munger? First, the points of view are mine, so I do not pretend I am right all the time; these are my conclusions and thoughts. The combination of Charlie Munger's and Warren Buffett's personalities give you a big picture. I believe Charlie Munger is a "reincarnation" of Benjamin Franklin. The importance of choosing the "right heroes" for yourself has been very clear for both Charlie Munger and Warren Buffett. As Warren Buffett put it in his interview: "It is a terrible thing to be let down by your heroes[xi]."

To understand Charlie better, I suggest you read more about Benjamin Franklin, who was a genius with a multidisciplinary education and a wide range of talents. What is ethics for Charlie Munger? Charlie is sure that you could get much more money and a better reputation in business and life from honesty. "Conduct yourself in life so other people trust you. It helps even more if they're right to trust you[xii]". (Charlie Munger, 2011 Berkshire Hathaway Meeting).

No other asset is more powerful than others having unconditional trust in you. Charlie's main principle in life is to invent the problem or matter to find the most logical answer or decision.

Life is not a very fair thing, but you could make it better, and it is not that difficult. To be happy, it is not enough to win a lottery for $1 million or to win an Oscar and marry a pretty woman or handsome man. Continuous learning and education gives you unlimited feeling of satisfaction and happiness.

# Charlie Munger Personal Characteristics: Rationality, Wisdom, Humanity, Sometimes Christlike Charlie

For value investors, to introduce Charlie is the same as to introduce the pope in the Vatican. This book is devoted to Charlie Munger, his values and morality, but in its very essence, this book is about mistakes, about failure.

I want this book to reflect Charlie Munger's individuality. I want to make this an interesting read, so I have put quotes by Charlie into a dialogue with modern businesspeople and Wall Street traders. Sometimes I see Charlie Munger as being a mirror, sometimes a reflection of my grandfather or myself. Some parts of his character and values cross with mine. The reader may ask what exactly is so common between us. Well, maybe the love for children, the faith in humility, discipline, and all parts of my philosophy of life.

You could argue Charlie Munger is not a person of the modern world. I am not saying he is an ideal man, but as a writer, I believe I have the right to exaggerate my hero and compare him with others.

An epiphany occurred to me when I watched Hans Holbein painting *Christ in the Tomb of Hans Holbein, it was made in 1521*[xiii]. If you observe the painting for several minutes, you have a feeling of losing the feeling of fear and a shock; it is depressing to watch it. It is rarely good picture I think only few artist have ever exposed it so. You can google to watch it or go to Basle, Kunstmuseum, Switzerland.

At the same time, I was thinking what Charlie Munger would do in my place. He is not influenced by emotions; he would probably never lose his feeling of confidence. That is one of the rare qualities Charlie Munger possesses: a quiet mind and a tendency to assess the world with objectivity. That is why Warren Buffett likes him so much.

As I am not a professional writer. Do you know how hard it is to be a writer, to carry such a responsibility? I allow myself to compare Charlie

Munger with Jesus Christ. I would like to get this book to be used by the next generations to study Charlie Munger for another hundred years.

Sometimes I picture Charlie Munger as rational, compassionate, and humble—even "Christlike Charlie." The main idea of the book is to picture Charlie as a positively good and wise man, his contrarianism and unemotionality. Nowadays this is the biggest problem ever; it is difficult to find such a unique personality. I think Charlie Munger is a good person only because he is at the same time ridiculously direct; he is funny and enjoys success because of this. He got my sympathy as a good man because he is a genius of our time whose ideas and standards of humanity and morality could influence our society. An image of a "positively good man" is of course in confrontation with a modern value system. The contemporary world is concentrated with the evils of materialism, egoism, poor ethnics and morals, and ethics of self-interest and personal worth. This is exactly the point of my introducing you to Charlie Munger. I idealize the figure of Charlie and sometimes exaggerate his human qualities, but as discussed with my dear readers, I am doing my best to present you my portrait of Charlie Munger, who is one of the most intellectual people of our time.

The central topic of our discussion is capitalism, which is evident in the important role played by money in "Charlie and Devils." The story reflects spirits, poverty, and luck of morality and ethics of a modern man Wall Street trader. Mr. Brown is a Wall Street trader, who is seduced by everyday stock trading and easy money.

As you may know, Charlie is a billionaire, but it was not a sudden inherited fortune. The characters and personalities of this novel are money managers who have a different standard in life and who from time to time are vulgar, wrong, and very different from Charlie. However, not everybody is born perfect.

"Devils," as I describe modern money managers in my story, are a group of people with whom Charlie is usually in confrontation. The book therefore involves dramatic and confrontational discussions and dialogues with these "contemporary money managers" on lessons of life and morals. Some of the topics are about humanity.

I think that for Charlie Munger, capital allocation is a topic of huge importance, so he is clearly thinking through every decision using his mental model filters. He also spends a significant amount of time learning about the different industries to widen his circle of competence and mental models. But once that mental capital and time are expended, and the purchase of stock is made, a sell would in essence be a huge waste of his personal and mental resources.

Everyday speculation and trading do not matter much to Charlie or Buffett. You could also ask why I use this name "devils" for money managers. This is because there is an apocalyptic atmosphere about money and materialism. In this atmosphere, the ideas of Charlie Munger are tested. You may argue that Charlie Munger is a person from another world. He always keeps himself apart from all the noise around him. He spent his years reading and not feeling the pressure of contemporary life. Once in an interview he said that he never uses Twitter and does not have a cell phone. It is impossible for him to work under any pressure or under the authority of somebody else. However, for Warren Buffett he makes an exception. Now both men and their relationship have a well-worn pattern. According to many who know them, Charlie Munger plays the alpha role in every relationship in his life: with his family, in the law firm he founded, on the boards of companies he directs. However, not with Buffett. "That is one of the beauties of the partnership," Munger said in an interview. "I am in so many activities where I am the dominant personality. Yet [with Warren] I am particularly willing to play a secondary role. Warren is a more able man in doing what we are doing.

"It is not letting ego or jealously or your own personality take over. Intelligence takes over[xiv]."

Today Charlie Munger, a man of ninety-five, is full of energy and ideas. He never stops reading and learning. Sometimes you will see in a book that Charlie appears as a Christlike figure, preaching the values of truth, morality, compassion, and deep knowledge.

Charlie, in my book, has a teacher function. I was trying to find out how his values, morals, and ethics could have been incorporated into a modern world. He is a philosopher who came to teach us. At the same time, I believe all people who came to every Berkshire Hathaway annual meeting events held once a year, forty thousand people attended, came to watch Warren and Charlie talking not because they want to earn money or to know how much Berkshire has made this year. They came because they like to search for wisdom with an intellectual context. Charlie Munger is known as someone who never tells any lies; this innocence and independence help win the trust of those he meets. People are sick of negative qualities such as greed, mistrust, hatred, envy, and resentment. The honesty and truthfulness are what win him the friendship and loyalty of others, not only in the United States, but worldwide.

As you may know, Charlie has his own system, known as the "Psychology of Human Misjudgment,[xv]" and mental models. We will explore how these ideas and mistakes, which are very important, interact with each other. If you ignore them, you will be in many troubles and make mistakes throughout your lifetime.

This is enough by way of introduction. Enjoy your reading!

# Chapter One

## Charlie and Devils: The Story

It was a dark morning at the end of November; the train left from Omaha and was on the way to New York City. The weather was cloudy, dark, and rainy. There was a very different public inside of that train. Part of the people were ordinarily dressed, but you could also see many people in business attire. It was tight and crowded. People were tired. Some were sleeping, others reading, but everybody felt indifferent toward each other. In one of the train cars, two people were sitting. One happened to be a communicable person; dressed very nice, brown shoes and his jacket were old, as the fashion was in the 1960s. It was a man of thirty-five to forty years old.

Another man of seventy-two years old had gray hair—almost no hair at all—gray eyes, and a big and very serious face. No smile, but you have a feeling that the man had plenty of character, but was a kind and nice person and was humble, human—you feel it. He was dressed very formally; his clothes were those of a businessperson, and you feel the material was of good quality, made of wool, as if it was a very expensive suit. You could say there was something special in the face of this man.

The eyes of the old man were clear his cheeks were sunken, his nose was small, and he was wearing glasses. His glasses model could tell you that he did not care for fashion, and you might notice he was a continuous lifelong learner and reader. The man had a book in his hand, but it was too dark to see which one.

The young person happened to be a young Wall Street trader named Mr. Brown.

He turned to his neighbor and said, "Is it another cold day today."

"Very," replied shortly, the other person, who was disturbed during his reading. However, at the same time he understood that he was in a train with others and could easily be disturbed. The dialogues were fast, impossible to avoid.

"You seem to like a long trip."

Charlie Munger was not answering; he looked preoccupied with his reading. At that right moment he does not want to speak, it was noisy, this entire crowd around him. Nobody knew if he was listening at all to what was happening around him.

The young man was very persistent and showed his will to continue a dialogue.

"But permit me. May I introduce myself?" said the young man. "My name is David Brown." Charlie stopped reading for a moment and promptly looked the man in his eyes.

"Charlie Munger," he responded very politely.

"Oh, Charlie Munger. I do not know you, sir, but I cannot say I never heard your name before. You are a partner of Warren Buffett of Berkshire Hathaway, right?"

## Success Means Being a Learning Machine

Charlie was thinking this was the last time he took a train for such a long trip. He could avoid all of these stupid conversations, but now it was too late, and he could not run away from it. Almost two hours more to New York.

Mr. Brown: "Ha, ha, ha. Such luck, to meet such an intelligent person, in such a situation, reading on the train. Could not be better company. I heard you are a learning machine. You have a multidisciplinary knowledge, with all of the mental tricks and models anticipating, of course, opinion, and trading money every day. I also heard you have your own models of human misjudgment, models of psychology, which you use in your everyday life. Wonderful, wonderful writing! Such a luck!

"I heard about you a lot. What exactly are you studying for, Charlie? Are you to become a professor in value investing?"

"Yes, I studied. Have you ever heard of Kopmeyer?" He said, "The best investment you can make is in you"[xvi]. I am a continuous self-learner, and it is a lot of fun. What about you?"

"No. Well, I've never studied anything," Mr. Brown answered. "Why are you doing it, Charlie?"

Charlie: "Wisdom acquisition is a moral duty. It's not something you do just to advance in life. As a corollary to that proposition which is very important, it means that you are hooked for lifetime learning. And without lifetime learning, you people are not going to do very well. You are not going to get very far in life based on what you already know. You're going to advance in life by what you learn after you leave here. I constantly see people rise in life who are not the smartest, sometimes not even the most diligent, but they are learning machines. They go to bed every night a little wiser than they were when they got up and boy does that help, particularly when you have a long run ahead of you[xvii]".

Mr. Brown: "Well, you know, it is not so easy to speak this nicely. Words of wisdom, wisdom acquisitions, if you are already rich. I know you have your billons. You know what, you...you will get nothing. I would not give you...fifty cents if you just speak your nice words only. You know, at one time I was like you. I am hosting a dinner in New York City tonight, one charity event. Please come, so we can have a longer conversation with each other."

Charlie politely answered: "I have a long meeting today, but I will try come to your event."

Mr. Brown: "Are you a greater admirer of the female sex, Charlie? Tell me in advance."

Charlie: "I am. No! Perhaps you do not know, but I am married. I am a very rational human. I was born with it. Some people are born with different qualities, but what they gave me is rationality[xviii]."

Mr. Brown: "Well, it is true, you are a such holy person, Mr. Munger, and God loves the fellow like you."

Charlie was thinking about his rationality and remembered a story. Once Charlie was sitting with a beautiful woman and she asked, What is the secret of your success? I am rational, he told her. Why should he continue to speak with this person? Charlie's conversation usually was simple, straightforward, and logical; however, the more absurd it became in the present instance.

Mr. Brown: "Could I kindly ask you, dear Charlie, What are the reasons for your success in life? You have been asked that questions before, so tell me about it more please."

"Well, I realized very early I was never going to succeed as a movie star or other. My grandfather provided me an idea that my main duty is to become as rational as I can be. I was not good at anything else, so I steered into something that worked well for me. Confucius said we have a moral duty to rationality; that is why I like him so much. I had the same idea years ago. Berkshire is a temple of rationality[xix]."

Charlie had a faint blush come into his pale face, remembering that it was not always so easy all the time, though his voice was no louder than before.

"Worldly wisdom acquisition is a moral duty," he told Mr. Brown. "Of course, if you are the sort of honest and principled fellow that your words seem to indicate, there will not be any difficulties between us. Such an honor to know you, Mr. Munger. Goodbye for now, and hope to see you very soon."

Charlie left the train, which had arrived at a crowded New York City central station. Meanwhile he was thinking about whether he really wanted to join Mr. Brown's charity event in the evening. He looked and spoke like a very interesting person. Charlie thought who knows why he wants to speak, why he was sitting next to him in this train.

In the meantime, Mr. Brown arrived an hour early to check that his charity event was organized the right way. He hated to be disappointed. He hated when something was missing, the small details like the wrong flowers in the lobby where the main event would be held. He would have to check everything. The main idea was to keep the most prominent and richest people together for them to make donations for a hospital in New York City. A lot of Wall Street people, mostly bankers, and some celebrities would be there tonight. But he was thinking about this exceptional person, Mr. Munger. Would he come tonight?

The people started to arrive in the main hall; he met his friend Mr. Arnold and told him.

Mr. Brown: "You are going to be very surprised who is going to be here tonight. Do you know Charlie Munger, the person who is a partner with Buffett at Berkshire Hathaway? He is not very often at events like this. You have to speak with him tonight; he has a very direct personality but sometimes is so honest and direct, almost as a child—very well educated, though. He is highly intellectual, but sometimes too direct, you know. But here he is! Dear gentlemen, may I introduce Charlie Munger?"

Mr. Brown: "Charlie, such an honor you came here to join us tonight."

One blond man, twenty-seven years old, standing next to Charlie turned and asked, "Dear Charlie, you always tell people they have to expect only a few really worthy insights in value investing to make a bet heavily and seldom, several time in a lifetime. What do you mean? How does it work to bet big when they come along? If you don't mind, please give me some practical examples."

### Be Patient No Matter How Much Time It Takes

Charlie: "If you took the top ten decisions out, we have a pretty average record. It wasn't hyperactivity, but a hell of a lot of patience. You stuck to your principles and when opportunities came along, you pounced on them with a vigor. With all that vigor, you only made a decision every two years. We do more deals now, but it happened with relatively few decisions and staying the course for decades and holding our fire until something came along worth doing.

"And the wise ones bet heavily when the world offers them that opportunity. They bet big when they have the odds. And the rest of the time, they don't. It's just that simple[xx]."

After a while Charlie continued: "Well, here we do have a practical example, I read *Barron's* for fifty years. In fifty years, I found one investment opportunity in *Barron's* out of which I made about $80 million with almost no risk. I took the $80 million and gave it to Li Lu, who turned it into $400 or $500 million. So, I have made $400 or $500 million reading *Barron's* for fifty years and following one idea. Now that doesn't help you very much, does it? I'm sorry, but that's the way it really happened. If you can't do it…I didn't have a lot of ideas. I didn't find them that easily, but I did pounce on one[xxi]."

The blond young man and others also listed with a fair amount of interest.

"I didn't expect it would be easy, but I also have in mind a diversification. What are your thoughts on that?"

Charlie: "The Berkshire-style investors tend to be less diversified than other people. The academics have done a terrible disservice to intelligent investors by glorifying the idea of diversification. Because I just think the whole concept is literally almost insane"[xxii].

"A lot of other people are trying to be brilliant, and we are just trying to be rational[xxiii]."

He speaks so well—indeed, very well, everyone was thinking.

## Charlies Grandfather. As His Role Model

Mr. Brown: "Help yourself, Charlie. Could you tell us where you were born and raised? I want to know everything! You interest me greatly."

Charlie: "I think you count on more booms and busts over your remaining lifetime. How big and with what cyclicality I can't tell you. I can tell you the best way of coping, which is just to put your head down and behave credibly every day. I will say something about life generally. I was lucky. I had an ancestor who I never met. My mother's grandfather was a pioneer who came out to Iowa and lived in a small house with his young wife. It was a cave. He literally was a pioneer coming from nothing and rose to control the leading bank in the town. He would give away nothing by himself, but my great grandmother made him a generous man, and he gave a lot back to society. Having wrested this success from troubles and struggles, he had this theory looking back at his long life. He owned farms at the end, and he leased them to Germans. You can't lose money leasing to Germans. He believed that real opportunities that come to you are few. Most people just get a few times to make a difference, when you find one and you can clearly recognize it. Seize it boldly and don't do it small. My mother transmitted this to me as part of family quirks, though she wasn't interested in finance. Of course, this guy was my soul mate - the great grandfather I never knew. I have totally adopted his point of view, I must say it has worked wonderfully. So I quit claim my great grandfathers' rule to you - assume your really major opportunities in life are going to be few and when you get a lollapalooza for god's sake don't hang by like a timid little rabbit. Don't hang back - there aren't that many of the really big good ones[xxiv]".

### Learning and Patience Will Pay off in Unexpected Ways

Charlie thanked him for the great question. Everybody around the table enjoyed listening to Charlie with great interest.

The man who was very quiet said, "Once I read a story about you, dear Charlie. Perhaps you can remember these funny stories of you and calculators and the dean of the Mathematics Department of the university."

Charlie: "OK, now the story. When I was in the first-year calculus course at my university, we had a special treat: the dean of the Mathematics Department was teaching our class. On the first day of class, he said that while we could use graphing calculators, he discouraged them, saying they would ultimately inhibit our learning and lower our grade. No other comments were made all year on this. Well, of course, I disregarded this comment, arguing I was never going to need calculus again, and took the easy way out. When I showed up for the final exam, there was a note on the first page saying, "Calculators are not permitted[xxv]."

Everyone burst out laughing. Charlie was laughing himself.

Mr. Brown: "I am glad you can laugh about it. It was not very funny for everybody except you, I believe. I can see you are a most good-natured man."

"Not always," Charlie replied.

"But I am," Mr. Brown answered unexpectedly. "If you want to know, I am always a good-hearted person. It was always like that, and today I am here to support this charity event, but as a trader I very often lose my temper, I start to be angry too quickly. Before you came—"

Another man interrupted. "Please go on, Charlie. You can remember some more stories. I still don't know any person who can tell the story straight like that. Your Berkshire annual meeting comments every year are fantastic."

Mr. Brown: "You have to understand, folks: Charlie is extremely clever, at least ten times more than we are all together. Nevertheless, could you tell us more about the problems of Berkshire—your failures, your mistakes—please? You said recently we have to go for a 'no-brainer decisions' margin of safety and keep things simple?"

Charlie: "We have no system for having automatic good judgment on all our investment decisions that can be made. Ours is a totally different system. We just look for a no-brainer decision. As Buffett and I say over and over again, we don't leap seven-foot fences. Instead, we look for one-foot fences with big rewards on the other side. So, we've succeed by making the world easy for ourselves, not by solving hard problems[xxvi]."

Mr. Brown: "But how can you guys win fast all the time, instead of losing?"

Charlie: "Any par can see that a horse carrying a light weight with a wonderful win rate and a good postposition, et cetera, et cetera, is way more likely to win than a horse with a terrible record and extra weight and so on and so on. But if you look at the odds, the bad horse pays a hundred to one, whereas the good horse pays three to two. Then it's not clear which is statistically the best bet using the mathematics of Fermat and Pascal. The prices have changed in such a way that it's very hard to beat the system.

And then the track is taking 17 percent off the top. So not only do you have to outwit all the other betters, but you've got to outwit them by such a big margin that on average, you can afford to take 17 percent of your gross bets off the top and give it to the house before the rest of your money can be put to work. Given those mathematics, is it possible to beat the horses only using one's intelligence? Intelligence should give some edge, because lots of people who don't know anything go out and bet lucky numbers and so forth. Therefore, somebody who really thinks about nothing but horse performance and is shrewd and mathematical could have a very considerable edge, in the absence of the frictional cost caused by the house take.

Unfortunately, what a shrewd horseplayer's edge does in most cases is to reduce his average loss over a season of betting from the 17 percent that he would lose if he got the average result to maybe 10 percent. However, there are actually a few people who can beat the game after paying the full 17 percent. I used to play poker when I was young with a guy who made a substantial living doing nothing but bet harness races.

Now, harness racing is a relatively inefficient market. You don't have the depth of intelligence betting on harness races that you do on regular races. What my poker pal would do was to think about harness races as his main profession. And he would bet only occasionally when he saw some mispriced bet available. And by doing that, after paying the full handle to the house—which I presume was around 17 percent—he made a substantial living. You have to say that's rare. However, the market was not perfectly efficient. And if it weren't for that big 17 percent handle, lots of people would regularly be beating lots of other people at the horse races. It's efficient, yes. But it's not perfectly efficient. And with enough shrewdness and fanaticism, some people will get better results than others.

The stock market is the same way—except that the house handle is so much lower. If you take transaction costs—the spread between the bid and the ask plus the commissions—and if you do not trade too actively, you are talking about fairly low transaction costs. So that with enough fanaticism and enough discipline, some of the shrewd people are going to get way better results than average in the nature of things. It is not a bit easy. And, of course, 50 percent will end up in the bottom half, and 70 percent will end up in the bottom 70 percent. But some people will have an advantage. And in a fairly low transaction cost operation, they will get better-than-average results in stock picking.

How do you get to be one of those who is a winner—in a relative sense—instead of a loser? Here again, look at the pari-mutuel system. I had dinner last night by absolute accident with the president of Santa Anita. He says that there are two or three betters who have a credit arrangement with them, now that they have off-track betting, who are actually beating the house. They're sending money out net after the full handle—a lot of it to Las Vegas, by the way—to people who are actually winning slightly, net, after paying the full handle. They're that shrewd about something with as much unpredictability as horse racing."

## Big Ideas Need Time

"And the one thing that all those winning betters in the whole history of people who've beaten the pari-mutuel system have is quite simple. They bet very seldom. It's not given to human beings to have such talent that they can just know everything about everything all the time. But it is given to human beings who work hard at it—who look and sift the world for a mispriced bet—that they can occasionally find one. And the wise ones bet heavily when the world offers them that opportunity. They bet big when they have the odds. And the rest of the time, they don't. It's just that simple.

That is a very simple concept. And to me it's obviously right—based on experience not only from the pari-mutuel system, but everywhere else. And yet, in investment management, practically nobody operates that way. We operate that way—I'm talking about Buffett and Munger. And we're not alone in the world. But a huge majority of people have some other crazy construct in their heads. And instead of waiting for a near cinch and loading up, they apparently ascribe to the theory that if they work a little harder or hire more business school students, they'll come to know everything about everything all the time[xxvii]."

Mr. Brown: "Oh really, it is all about thinking philosophy. Maybe Charlie is a philosopher who came to teach us, and who knows, perhaps he really does mean to teach people. I think it is possible, Charlie. Will you agree that your philosophy of capital allocation and worldly wisdom is the same as Warren Buffett's philosophy? He is your longtime partner. Once I saw him speaking. He is so humble, and he told us that money is not that important in life, and he has all the money in the world, you know. But it is not possible—nobody could live happily these days here in New York City without cash, champagne, and beautiful women."

## Stay Rational and Lower Your Expectations

Charlie: "The secret of happiness is to lower your expectations. You have to be aware of beautiful women as well. They could easily manipulate you. I want to tell you the story of what happened with me once. The manipulation still works even though you know you're doing it. And I've seen that done by one person to another. I drew this beautiful woman as my dinner partner a few years ago, and I'd never seen her before. Well, she's married to a prominent Angelino, and she sat down next to me, and she turned her beautiful face up and she said, "Charlie." She said, "What one word accounts for your remarkable success in life?" And I knew I was being manipulated and that she'd done this before, and I just loved it. I mean I never see this woman without a little lift in my spirits. And by the way, I told her I was rational. You'll have to judge yourself whether that's true. I may be demonstrating some psychological tendency I hadn't planned on demonstrating[xxviii]."

Everybody started to laugh, but not a young blond person who was standing next to Charlie.

"Have you finished talking?" asked the blond man. Charlie suddenly fell silent. Everyone waited for him to go on to draw some conclusions. You never know what Charlie is thinking. When he is silent, it feels as if he enjoys communicating with himself first.

"So, it follows from your example that one can't really live one's life on animal spirits and instincts? But it is just impossible, for some reason," Mr. Brown said.

Charlie again looked around the table, with an earnest and searching look: "Are you angry with me for all of these lectures?" He was managing to look everyone straight in the eye.

"What for?" cried the blond man, astonished. "We are lucky to have you here."

Charlie: "Well, because I keep lecturing you…"

Everyone laughed.

"Ok, please don't worry, dear Charlie, about lecturing us".

Now the wife of somebody's guest started to speak: "Well now, will you be so kind to tell us how you feel about your famous work, "The Psychology of Human Misjudgment"? Particularly of my interest is something about self-pity as a terrible way to behave. But that is not so easy, Charlie. We all would like to be a 'sympathy seeker' when we have a big problem."

### Self-Pity Is Annoying and Counterproductive

Charlie stared at her in astonishment.

Charlie said, "Self-pity can get pretty close to paranoia, and paranoia is one of the very hardest things to reverse. You do not want to drift into self-pity. I had a friend who carried a big stack of linen-based cards. And when somebody would make a comment that reflected self-pity, he would slowly and portentously put out this huge stack of cards, take the top one and hand it to the person, and the card said, 'Your story has touched my heart. Never have I heard of anyone with as many misfortunes as you.' Well you can say that's wiggery, but I suggest it can be mental hygiene. Every time you find you're drifting into self-pity, whatever the case—even if your child is dying of cancer, self-pity is not going to help—just give yourself one of my friend's cards. Self-pity is always counterproductive. It's the wrong way to think. And when you avoid it, you get a great advantage over everybody else, or almost everybody else, because self-pity is a standard response. And you can train yourself out of it[xxix]."

Mr. Brown: "Somebody said that this world does not have a very good reputation for treating its temporary occupants with tender loving care. So, if you want to invoke sympathy (and be a sympathy seeker), you will not lack opportunities. But if we are to cope with our problems, we need sympathy and more determination. Well, this is so hard. You seem to be an emotional control freak; you are able to control all your thoughts and actions Charlie. I have been in business during the recession times. It could not be worse, all of this pressure. What do you think of it, Charlie?"

Charlie: "As for the recession, I think you should all just say 'So what?' There are good times and bad times. And we know from the example of other people that if you constantly stand well by your generation and cope with competency and grace with whatever life deals you and keep doing it, your share of the honors and emoluments of the civilization in due time are very likely to come."

"Well, all right," Mr. Brown said, "but if you are such an expert on psychology and morals, how could we deal with a crazy situation—with crazy people who want to break you, break your personality with all the methods existing?"

## Nobody Is a Victim. Fix It and Move On

Charlie: "Whenever you think something or some person is ruining your life, it's you. A victimization mentality is debilitating. It is actually you who are ruining your life. Feeling like a victim is a perfectly disastrous way to go through life. If you just take the attitude that however bad it is in any way, it's always your fault and you just fix it as best you can—the so-called "iron prescription"—I think that really works[xxx]."

Mr. Brown responded, "You know, Charlie, many years ago I read your biography. I think, well I have an impression you are a very happy person both with business and family. I was reading that you have many children at home. There are eight children. In addition, you spent all of your life being a learning machine, a voracious reader. You are a very special person, and I see you are seeking the truth and logic at all of Berkshire's annual meetings and events. Now I am myself, your biggest fan and follower. You used to tell shareholders everything; you keep nothing back. And of course, all the time people are angry with you because you can't lie, so you get a lot of enemies as well."

"You get a lot of enemies because of your rationality, your principles in life. It looks like it is so easy for you. What do you have to be afraid of? You can afford to tell your shareholders the truth, explain the decision-making, answering their most complex of questions. I could not tell everything—even to my own children, to win their trust and respect. People trust you and Warren. And this truth is extremely valuable advice in difficult times. You are this way because of your soul; you have a great family and old values. Through your contact with children, you are also a warm-hearted person, Charlie.

"I like children myself a lot, especially when they are young, and could not lie—these small beauties, so honest, direct, sometimes laughing, full of energy, running around, and when you see them, you feel excellent. You forget about a feeling of depression. Therefore, I understand you, dear Charlie. Once I was waiting for an important deal to come. I was sitting on in a train as we had done some days ago with Charlie and I thought; 'Now I am on the way to be with all of these people. I have to behave honestly and firmly. I have to be polite and open with everyone. Perhaps all of them will look at me and think I am too simple, too direct, that I am stupid and losing my mind. Everybody hates a messenger.'"

## First Conclusion Bias Are Failures

"I often think like that. I think it is a habit; we all have to be trained to speak the truth, which is so uncommon. By the way, dear Charlie, how were you able to cultivate and maintain great mental habits to change your conclusion on certain matters? It seems you have a huge advantage!"

Charlie: "It is easy to see that a quickly reached conclusion, triggered by doubt-avoidance tendency, when combined with a tendency to resist any change in that conclusion, will naturally cause a lot of errors in cognition for modern man. And so, it observably works out. We all deal much with others whom we correctly diagnose as imprisoned in poor conclusions that are maintained by mental habits they formed early and with carry to their graves. So great is the bad-decision problem caused by inconsistency avoidance tendency that our courts have adopted important strategies against it. For instance, before making decisions, judges and juries are required to hear long and skillful presentations of evidence and argument from the side they will not naturally favor, given their ideas in place. And this helps prevent considerable bad thinking from 'first conclusion bias.' Similarly, other modern decision makers will often force groups to consider skillful counterarguments before making decisions[xxxi]."

"Yes, but we are not getting this approach of worldly wisdom, or mental models with a multidisciplinary approach, from our universities. Should one develop his own mental models, a system of thinking? Please help to explain it better," said Mr. Brown.

Charlie: "So if your professor won't give you an appropriate multidisciplinary approach, if each wants to overuse his own models and underuse the important models in other disciplines—you can correct that folly yourself. Just because he is a horse patriot, you don't have to be one, too. You can reach out and grasp the model that better solves the overall problem. All you have to do is know it and develop the right mental habits[xxxii]."

Mrs. Brown: "Charlie, you are extremely clever. I still do not see how anybody could tell better stories honestly like that."

Charlie left the table to meet his acquaintances in another hall. People on the table started to talk:

"He is nice and an extremely intelligent person, but a bit on the simple side, too direct. It is hilarious."

"Yes, rather," answered another guy.

"That is the reason for his personal success and Berkshire's success; he seems a straight talker like Warren Buffett himself. But Charlie is special; his direct approach makes him a bit ridiculous even. Simple, maybe, but he has all his wit and wisdom—the best sense of course. Exactly like me," said Mr. Brown.

Charlie returned to his seat around the table. An old man who was sitting not so far from him asked, "Listen, Charlie, I have an enormous favor to ask of you. Don't you think that habits are our destiny? Maybe one is already born to have a speculative nature. I don't think I am able to change myself ever."

## Not Everyone Can Be a Rational Thinker. But You Can

Charlie: "The brain of man conserves programming space by being reluctant to change, which is a form of inconsistency avoidance. We see all sorts of these human habits, constructive and destructive. Few people can list a lot of bad habits that they have eliminated, and some people cannot identify even one of these. I asked; practically everyone has a great many bad habits he has long maintained despite there being too much in many cases to appraise early-formed habits as destiny. When Marley's miserable host says 'I wear the chains I forged in life,' he is talking about chains of habits that were too light to be felt before they became too strong to be broken[xxxiii]."

Mr. Brown: "Dear Charlie, lets change the topic. You know, Charlie, I like you a lot, and I like our discussion about moral and values. I have to tell you one story that happened to me recently, but this is a very private story between you and me. I met a girl in Las Vegas, she looked so beautiful, and I fell in love with her. She is very different from all the girls I ever met before."

"The worst-case scenario," Charlie was thinking, though his face expressed nothing.

Mr. Brown: "You know Charlie, New York is a city of comforts and luxuries. You could not imagine how easily luxurious habits are adopted and how difficult it is to get rid of them. You know, little by little they have become necessities—to buy a Chagall picture, and they are so beautiful, I have two of them. So, if you are professional in life, you do not get any time for yourself at all. New York is very busy—meetings stress. How do you find time to learn about these models and doing whatever else interests you? How do you find time to do fun things besides learning?"

Charlie: "I've always taken a fair amount of time to do what I really wanted to do—some of which was merely to fish or play bridge or play golf. Each of us must figure out his or her own lifestyle. You may want to work seventy hours a week for ten years to make partner at Cravath and thereby often obtain the obligation to do more of the same. Or you may say, 'I am not willing to pay that price.' Either way, it's a totally personal decision that you have to make by your own lights.

"But whatever you decide, I think it's a huge mistake not to absorb elementary worldly wisdom if you're capable of doing it because it makes you better able to serve others. It makes you better able to serve yourself, and it makes life more fun. So, if you have an aptitude for doing it, I think you'd be crazy not to. Your life will be enriched—not only financially, but in a host of other ways—if you do[xxxiv]."

Mr. Brown: "Yes, Charlie, this is the correct idea. Are you in effect fulfilling your responsibility to share the wisdom that you've acquired over the years?"

Charlie: "Sure, look at Berkshire Hathaway. I call it the ultimate didactic enterprise. Warren's never going to spend any money. He is going to give it back to society. He is just building a platform so people will listen to his notions. Needless to say, they are very good notions. And the platform is not bad either. But you could argue that Warren and I are academics in our own way."

Mr. Brown: "Yes, I quite agree with you: this is an amazing example, but dear Charlie, back to the question. How did you balance reading that much and having so many children?"

### How to Read 24/7

Charlie: "When I want to read something, I turn everything else down. I don't know a wise person who doesn't read a lot. I think people who multitask pay a huge price—they can't think of everything deeply, giving the world the advantage, which they shouldn't give. I wouldn't successfully be doing it. I did not succeed in life by intelligence—I succeeded because I have a long attention span[xxxv]."

At this point two people came to their table. Everybody stopped talking at once. Charlie remained in his chair next to Mr. Brown. It was quite late, about midnight. Some guests started to leave the event. He was thinking, it was enough discussions for today; this long day had to finish very soon. That was the only wish he had, as tomorrow there would be an important meeting. He again thought about the situation and crisis with Salomon Brothers, which they were dealing with at Berkshire right now. This is why he came here to New York City; all his thoughts now were focusing on it. Now he wanted to be alone in his hotel and rethink it again.

Charlie turned to Mr. Brown and said, "I am delighted to meet you, Mr. Brown. It was a very pleasant event and evening. Right now, I have to go. Excuse me."

Mr. Brown: "Charlie, our charity event is almost finished. I wish I would see you again very soon. Goodbye then. I expect you are very busy in New York City these days, but it was an enormous pleasure to speak with you. I am very happy to meet you in person, Charlie. I believe that God has brought you from Omaha to New York just for my sake. You may have other things to attend too, but I am the main reason. Goodbye."

All guests around the table were very pleased. It could not have been a better evening!

## Set High Standards. Honesty. Discipline. Salomon
## Brothers and Charlie

Soon Charlie was in his hotel room. He knew that tomorrow was going to be different from the usual working day at Berkshire—indeed very different from the ordinary reading and thinking. They, Buffett and he, had to act intelligent and diligent. Charlie's mind was preoccupied with thoughts. However, he knew the best thing in the world is to count on your own resources. This is what they did here at Berkshire. Buffett and he were rich enough to avoid a complex and difficult problem solving. They just wanted to sleep well at night. They hated to be disturbed by the noise around, the pressure of the crowd; it had been on this news all around. But financial conflict is exactly what they want to avoid in life. Buffett is just crazy about any harm to his international reputational risk. Everybody knows he said once, "Lose the money, and I will forgive you. Lose the reputation of the company, and I will be nasty[xxxvi]."

As sudden as it was, Charlie got a call the previous week from Buffett that the situation with Salomon Brothers was escalating, and they had to find the right strategy to act. To describe it shortly, Buffett was very scared these days; it was stress and pressure from government and it may cause a financial crisis around the world. Charlie was wondering if it was correct that Buffett was involved with Salomon Brothers. Warren Buffett got a call from the CEO of Salomon Brothers about an emergency issue; the management of the company had been accused of submitting false bids in an attempt to purchase more treasury bonds than permitted by one buyer. When Warren got a call from CEO John Gutfreund, who said that he was going to resign, Warren had to step in as the next CEO of Salomon Brothers.

Charlie's mind was polarized with thoughts: "You are never going to have perfect behavior in the miasma of easy money. When the financial scene starts reminding you of Sodom and Gomorrah, you should fear practical consequences even if you would like to participate in what is going on.

"Investment banking at the height of this last folly was a disgrace to the surrounding civilization[xxxvii]."

"You should have personal standards that are way better than the criminal law requires. Why should the criminal law determine your behavior? It would be crazy. Who would behave that way in marriage, or in partnership, or anything else? Why should you do it in your general dealing? I think this is a mess, and, of course, it's a little dispiriting to find that many of the people who are the worst miscreants don't have much sense of shame and are trying to go back as much as they can to the old behavior. The truth of the matter is, once you've shouted into the phone, 'I'll take x and y,' and three days later, you have an extra five million— once that has happened, the people just become hopeless addicts, and they lose their bearings[xxxviii]."

This is my interpretation of the Salomon Brothers story. What I want you to pay attention to is the way of thinking for both Charlie Munger and Warren Buffett in this situation. As we know from articles and newspapers, they both were under enormous pressure. They spoke long on the telephone with each other and trusted people, discussing the issue. Charlie came to New York City to be present at meetings with Buffett, to support him wherever he could. This situation demonstrated how these two great minds work so well together in a conflict situation. When Warren received a call about the situation at Salomon, he was not prepared to act, and it is usually very difficult to surprise him. On very short notice, it was difficult to appoint a new management director. It was also not very easy to find a correct person to manage this complex issue.

### If You Are Not Honest, It Is Not Them; It Is You

Warren Buffett described the process of finding the right person who could deal with the situation on behalf of the management of Salomon Brothers during this crisis: "I wasn't looking for Forrest Gump, either. But the dozen or so had all the IQ necessary; they had all the drive necessary. These are people who were used to working twelve-hour days and had lots of push. So, it was not a question of energy. It was a question of who, in my view, with both of those qualities already a given, really was the highest quality individual. It was the person who would not stick a gun to my head after he took the job, because I couldn't afford to fire whoever came in, and I couldn't afford to have him quit on me when the going got tough a week or two weeks or a month later, because with one more event like that, it would have been curtains. So, I really had to be sure of the steadfastness of the individual. I had to be sure he was up to it temperamentally because the pressure would be enormous.

"The person I decided on never asked me then, he never asked me a week later, he never asked me a month later, what the pay was. Basically, he was a battlefield promotion and he behaved like it was a battlefield promotion. He could have come to me and said, 'Look, I could go to Goldman Sachs and make $x$ this year, and this is going to be much tougher, so I want 150 percent of $x$ from you.' He never said a word about that. As a matter of fact, in the first year, just set on example, he reduced his pay, running the Tokyo office the year before. He never asked me to indemnify him against the lawsuits that would be forthcoming if the place failed. If things had gone bad, and you couldn't tell whether they would or not, we were going to get sued by everybody in the world. And, if Salomon had gone under, its indemnification would have been no good.

So, it would have been perfectly reasonable for this person to say, 'Well, look, I'll take this job but who knows what happened and if it happens, Salomon isn't going to be good for it. So, why doesn't Berkshire Hathaway or why don't you personally indemnify me against the lawsuits I'll be facing the rest of my life if this goes sour?'

"He never asked a word about it. It wasn't because he was dumb and didn't know enough to ask that. He just felt it was not the right timing to do it under these circumstances. So, in the end, I picked out an individual who I felt was an outstanding human being. He never let me down. He took on that job the next day. We come out of a directors' meeting at three in the afternoon. And there were these twelve people out there, and I just walked up to him and said to him, 'You're it, pal.' And, we went right from there down with the elevator to meet a couple hundred reporters who had come in on Sunday afternoon and who were plenty hostile in some ways. He set up there on up there on the stage with me and answered questions for three hours. I knew then I had made the right choice.

"Now, the interesting thing about that choice is that the qualities that attracted me to him were impossible for anyone to achieve. He didn't have to be able to jump seven feet. He didn't have to be able to throw a football sixty yard. He didn't have to remember every bridge hand he played the previous year or something of the sort. There was no feat of intellect or something like that. What he did was bring qualities like steadfastness and honesty. I knew he would tell me the bad news. I always worry about that with people who work for me. They don't need to tell me the good news. I just want to hear the bad news. I knew he would not get his ego involved in decisions. I knew he would not be envious or greedy or all of those things that they make people unattractive. And, the truth is, anybody can have those same qualities that Deryck Mangham, the fellow I picked, exhibited. They are not feats that are beyond anyone. They are simply a matter of deciding what are you going to do and what kind of person you are going to make out of yourself, and then doing it[xxxix]."

The Salomon office those days was extraordinary noisy and crowded. It seemed to Charlie as if the number of people was increasing with every minute, and more were still arriving. Voices were talking, and some people were stressed. Some were coming as if they were from the street, with coats and hats. They seemed to need each other's support that day. Nobody had an opinion of his own. To Charlie, they all seemed to be pushing one another. During the discussion, it was a strong feeling that nobody had a clear opinion: one was speaking, and the rest were just his supporters. Charlie was present, but parts of that dialogue were still missing. And that was very usual for him; he has an ability to switch off the noise of others when it is necessary, which was the case on that day. He was thinking, Why did this situation happen? At the same time, he was sure that only Warren Buffett, being present in all of those meetings, would save the company from a crash.

He was thinking, "Why does it happen? And now we get to Feuerstein, who was the general counsel with Salomon when John Gutfreund made his big error, and Feuerstein knew better. He told Gutfreund, "You have to report this as a matter of morality and prudent business judgment." He said, "It's probably not illegal; there's probably no legal duty to do it, but you have to do it as a matter of prudent conduct and proper dealing with your main customer." He said this to Gutfreund on at least two or three occasions. And he stopped. And, of course the persuasion failed, and when Gutfreund went down, Feuerstein went with him. It ruined a considerable part of Feuerstein's life.

Well Feuerstein, who was a member of the Harvard Law Review, made an elementary psychological mistake. You want to persuade somebody, you really tell them why. And what did we learn in lesson one? Incentives really matter? Vivid evidence really works? He should've told Gutfreund, "You're likely to ruin your life and disgrace your family and lose your money. And is Mozer worth this? I know both men. That would've worked. So, Feuerstein flunked elementary psychology, this very sophisticated, brilliant lawyer. But don't you do that. It's not very hard to do, you know, just to remember that 'Why?' is very important[xl]."

So many thoughts were in Charlie's mind; they couldn't believe that happened right now. As the meeting was over and Buffett announced the plan—what they were going to do and how it was going to happen—Charlie was sitting still. He was hoping that all of these people, this "entire family," would little by little disappear. Soon they would turn out to be nonexistent, and Buffett and he could calmly go down to discuss this matter personally. Disappointment, mistakes, faults, psychological denial, social proof—you name it.

Because of Warren Buffett being appointed CEO of Salomon Brothers the first year after John Feuerstein resigned and Charlie Munger being his trusted partner with almost unbelievable effort, Salomon Brothers was saved from bankruptcy.

## Older People Can Learn Too

The next day Charlie was meeting with Mr. Brown for lunch.

Mr. Brown: "Hey Charlie, nice to meet you again. Are you a modern-day stoic? But I am not like you; I'm a more emotional person. I was not sitting all the time at Wall Street. I have worked very hard all these years. I always took the money as reward and all of this nerve, talking nonstop, selling, and telling my client stories. By the way, what do you think about the poor employment market? It is hard to find a job for a lot of young people right now."

Charlie: "I tell you about an example of what I call a *real* bad employment market. My uncle Fred graduated from Harvard School of Architecture with great distinction and had a very successful practice during the 1920s, when he made over $10,000 a year. When the 1930s came, the architecture building permits dried up in Omaha. There was exactly zero work to do for architects, including my distinguishing architect uncle Fred. He moved to California and took drafting work at low rates for architects that still had some work…and when it got worse than that, he went to the country of Los Angeles. And in the country, they classified him as a laundry man to save money and had him do drafting work. He was always exercising his skill. He never complained but coped as best he could. His pay after deductions all through 1931 to 1934 was $101.08 per month.

When they created the FHA, he took the civil service exam and came first. For the rest of his life, he was the chief architect of the FHA in LA. He had a long and happy career doing that. He never got discouraged. He never thought what he had to do was something to wail about. In my long life, one should never feel sorry for yourself. If your child is dying of cancer, don't feel sorry for yourself. And the other thing you never want to have is envy. It's the only one of the deadly sins that you are never going to have any fun at all[xli]."

## Try to Remember Kipling's "If" and Move On

Charlie: "If you go through life just everlastingly plugging away at these bad times...you know Kipling has gone totally out of vogue because it is not politically correct to write lines like 'a woman is only a woman, but a good cigar is a smoke,' but Kipling's 'If' is still great poetry" 'If you can keep your mind while all others are losing theirs' is good advice for Wall Street and everywhere else. And he said treat the two imposters—success and failure—just the same. And in the end, he says, whatever else happens, 'you will be a man my son.' Good message, good message—why not take these opportunities/hardships to make a man of yourself? I know how you should cope with whatever the difficulties are—just keep your head down and do your best[xlii]."

## Keep Emotions Under Control. Just Fix it No Matter What it Takes

Mr. Brown: "But Charlie, may I ask you what you have to do with it all? You are the first man I have met in my whole life whom I can trust to speak with as a truly devoted friend. I believed in you from the first sight when we met on the train. But back to this beautiful woman from Las Vegas: I was losing my head because of her. It was so unfair how she dealt with me, but I could only thank her for this experience. She borrows $75,000, and I never see her again. I was in love with her, you know, started to drink, was ill for a long time, lost my business and money, and was in a misery for a long time. But after a while I was recovered, learned my lesson."

Charlie was looking in the man's eyes and said nothing. Mr. Brown was looking at him in silence: "Yes, correct, Charlie; it was silly to trust her. I am guilty myself. But it was so hard; she has manipulated me so easily." He was bitterly offended.

It was the beginning of November; the weather in New York City was unusually fine with some rain.

Mr. Brown turned to Charlie and said, "Enough mistakes! I have learned my lesson. There'll be no more of them from now on."

It has to be said at this point that the atmosphere between these two men was disagreeable.

Charlie: "There is no such thing as a problem-free life, but how we experience and react to our problems depends on us. Happiness is not a life without problems, but rather the strength to overcome the problems that come our way[xliii]."

Mr. Brown: "But I loved this woman. You're smiling, Charlie; you think I'm wrong."

Charlie: "I'm not smiling, but I do believe you're not quite right."

Mr. Brown: "Come on, Charlie, tell me straight out then: you believe 'not quite.'"

Charlie: "Yes, if you prefer then, you're totally wrong."

Mr. Brown: "If I prefer? You really believe I don't know that I was totally mistaken. It is my money and my decision. I am forcing into this circumstance. However, you, Charlie, know very little of emotions, of real life. I got much satisfaction when I helped this young woman with my money. After all, I believe one day she will come and give me my money back. You are smiling; you don't believe me? Right."

"It seems to me all this isn't really relevant to the matter at all," observed Charlie. "But let us change the topic."

Mr. Brown: "Well all right, let's talk about something different—for example, reading books. You have a reputation for being a learning machine. This is so fascinating to me. You devote your time not to focusing on business but on reading mostly. But still you have said you have eight children. Yes, people are multitasking these days trying to be perfect. It personally gives me an edge when people are not paying attention to reading and thinking. I am reading myself but not as much as I should. Most people nowadays are not paying attention to reading and thinking, and are instead on their Twitter and phones, posting what they have had for breakfast and lunch. This is how young people—and not only young—spend their time.

"I remember I read a *Fortune* magazine article with the title "Warren and Charlie and the Chocolate Factory[xliv]," where Warren gave you a great compliment. 'Warren Buffett: Charlie has read about as much as anybody I know. He is eighty-eight now, and when he is ninety-eight, he will remember everything he read. That's the difference. I read it and enjoy it, but I don't remember a damn thing.' Could you please explain it to me?"

## Invent the Method of Invention. Just Think It Backward

Charlie: "Alfred North Whitehead correctly said at one time that the rapid advance of civilization came only when man 'invented the method of invention.' He was referring to the huge growth in GDP per capita and many other good things we now take for granted. Big-time progress started a few hundred years ago. Before that, progress per century was almost nil. Just as civilization can progress only when it invents the method of invention, you can progress only when you learn the method of learning. I was very lucky. I came to law school having learned the method of learning, and nothing has served me better in my long life than continuous learning. Consider Warren Buffett again. If you watched him with a time clock, you'd find that about half of his working time is spent reading. Then a big chunk of the rest of the time is spent talking one on one, either on the telephone or personally, with highly gifted people whom he trusts and who trust him. Viewed up close Warren looks quite academic as he achieves worldly success."

Mr. Brown: "And reading is not everything, right? How you get an idea and knowledge to use to have a practical implementation? Let us call it a personal education story. How you get started?"

Charlie: "Next, my personal education history is interesting because its deficiencies and my peculiarities eventually created advantages. For some odd reason, I had an early and extreme multidisciplinary cast of mind. I couldn't stand waiting for a small idea in my own discipline when there was a big idea right over the fence in somebody else's discipline. So, I just grabbed in all directions for the big ideas that would really work. Nobody taught me to do that; I was just born with that yen. I also was born with a huge craving for synthesis. And when it didn't come easily, which was often, I would rag the problem, and then when I failed, I would put it aside, and I'd come back to it and rag it again. It took me twenty years to figure out why and how cult conversion methods worked. But the psychology departments haven't figured it out yet, so I'm ahead of them.

"But anyway, I have this tendency to want to rog the problems. Because World War II caught me, I drifted into some physics, and the Air Corps sent me to Caltech, where I did a little more physics as part of being made into a meteorologist. And there, at a very young age, I absorbed what I call the fundamental full attribution ethos of hard science. And that was enormously useful to me. Let me explain that ethos.

"Under this ethos, you've got to know all the big ideas in all the disciplines more fundamental than your own. You can never make any explanation that can be made in a more fundamental way, in any other way than the most fundamental way."

## Perfect Your Knowledge and Make a Big Bet

"And you always take with full attribution to the most fundamental ideas that you are required to use. When you're using physics, you say you're using physics. When you're using biology, you say you're using biology. And so on and so on. I could easily see that that ethos would get as a fine organizing system for my thought. And I strongly suspected that it would work very well in soft sciences as well as the hard sciences, so I just grabbed it all through my life in soft science as well as hard science. That was a lucky idea for me. Let me explain how extreme that ethos is in hard science. There is a constant, one of the fundamental constants in physics, called Boltzmann's constant. You probably all know it very well. And the interesting thing about Boltzmann's constant is that Boltzmann didn't discover it. So why is Boltzmann's constant now named for Boltzmann? Well, the answer is that Boltzmann derived that constant from basic physics in a more fundamental way than the poor forgotten fellow who found the constant in the first place in some less fundamental way. The ethos of hard science is so strong in favor of reductionism to the more fundamental body of knowledge that you can wash a discoverer right out of history when somebody else handled his discovery in a fundamental way. I think that is correct. I think Boltzmann's constant should be named for Boltzmann. At any rate, in my history and Berkshire's history, Berkshire went on and on into considerable economic success while ignoring the hard-form efficient morals doctrine once very popular in academic economics and ignoring the descendants of that doctrine in corporate finance where the results become even sillier than they were in economics. This naturally encouraged me.

"Finally, with my peculiar history, I'm also bold enough to be here today because at least when I was young, I wasn't a total klutz. For one year at the Harvard Law School, I was ranked second in a very large group, and I always figured that, while there were always a lot of people much smarter than I was, I didn't have to hang back totally in the thinking game[xlv]."

They talked in the manner of old friends. Mr. Brown's office was very dark at that moment. It was a big room, full of furniture of all kinds—office desks, cupboards, a broad red leather sofa, and paintings. On the table was tons of paper, both newspapers and books. Charlie was looking at the table, and on it were two or three books by Benjamin Graham, which were opened with some bookmarks visible. The oil paintings all around in that room created an atmosphere of smoke.

Mr. Brown: "Wall Street is a hard place to be, Charlie. You do not have the beautiful story of yours to sit and bet when you want to. You have enormous pressure from the clients. You behave how they want you to behave. You make commitments to buy some stocks. You make predictions. I feel myself close to an animal from time to time. Your beautiful stories on worldly wisdom and knowledge have nothing to do with practice. For a week or two, I did not eat, drink, or sleep. I never left this room. I was on my knees in front of the computer and watched as my stock portfolio was sinking every day with 80 percent. I thought, 'I'll die.' I was looking at myself and sitting in that chair all night long. No sleep. I could not forgive myself for feeling that stupid. I think you once told a fellow, "It is dishonorable to be stupider than you have to be.

"My honor was involved. I've never studied anything, you know. I am not so talented myself to have the discipline to do it. But you may see I have many books in my library today. But what I want to tell you is that this is all theory. It has nothing to do with practice and business. What about you, my friend? Could I kindly ask you, Charlie, how did you incorporate these models into a legal practice when you were a lawyer? And how did it work?"

## Mental Models to Deal with Reality

Charlie looked straight into his eyes and said, "Well, the models are there. But just as there are perverse incentives in academics, there are perverse incentives in law firms. In fact, in some respects, at law firms, it's much worse. Here is another model from law practice: When I was young, my father practiced law. One of his first friends—Grant McFayden, Omaha's pioneer Ford dealer—was a client. He was a perfectly marvelous man—a self-made Irishman who'd run away uneducated from a farm as a youth because his father beat him. So, he made his own way in the world. And he was a brilliant man of enormous charm and integrity—just a wonderful, wonderful man. In contrast, my father had another client who was a blow-hard, an overreaching, unfair, pompous, difficult man. And I must have been fourteen years old or thereabouts when I asked, 'Dad, why do you do so much work for Mr. X—this overreaching blowhard—instead of work-ing more for wonderful men like Grant McFayden?' My father said, 'Grant McFayden treats his employees right, his customers right, and his prob-lems right. And if he gets involved with a psychotic, he quickly walks over to where the psychotic is and works out an exit as fast as he can. Therefore, Grant McFayden doesn't have enough remunerative law to keep you in Coca Cola. But Mr. X is a walking minefield of wonderful legal business.'

"This case demonstrates one of the troubles of practicing law. To a considerable extent, you're going to be dealing with grossly defective people. They create an enormous amount of the remunerative law busi-ness. And even when your client is a paragon of virtue, you'll often be dealing with gross defectives on the other side or even on the bench. That's partly what drove me out of the profession. The rest was my own greed, but my success in serving greed partly allowed me to make easier the process of being honorable and sensible. Like Ben Franklin observed, 'It's hard for an empty sack to stand upright.' I'd argue that my father's model when I asked him about the two clients was a totally correct deduction. He taught me the right lesson. The lesson? As you go through life, sell your services once in a while to an unreasonable blowhard if that's what you must do to feed your family. But run your life like Grant McFayden. That was a great lesson. And he taught it in a very clever way—because instead of just pounding it in, he told it to me in a way that required a slight mental reach. And I had to make the reach myself in order to get an idea that I should behave like Grant McFayden. And because I had to reach for it, he figured Id hold it better. And, indeed, I've held it all the way through until today – through all of these decades. That's a very clever teaching method. There, again, we're talking about elementary psychology. It's elementary literature. Good literature makes the reader reach a little for understanding. That works better. You hold it better. It's a commitment and consistency tendency. If you've reached for it, the idea's pounded in better.

"As a lawyer or executive, you'll want to teach somebody what my father taught me, or maybe you'll want to teach them something else. And you can use lessons like this. Isn't that a great way to teach a child? My father used indirection on purpose. And look at how wonderfully it worked—like Captain Cook's wise use of psychology. I've been trying to imitate Grant McFayden ever since—for all my life. I may have had a few lapses. But at least I've been trying[xlvi]."

Mr. Brown: "You are so amusing, Charlie, so direct and honest. And all of these stories. Lawyers have much stronger financial incentives to represent a client who has problems like that, so they do see less interest in representing the people with highly ethical standards. Never ask the barber if you need a haircut.

"This story is so much fun; I have no wit like that. And if I had as much wit as you, I'd have just sat here today and not said a word. Allow me to ask your opinion, Charlie. I can't help thinking that Wall Street has so many more thieves in the world than non-thieves, and the supremely honest man who has never stolen anything or manipulated the peo- ple's opinion on selling risky stock or anything like that in our life simply doesn't exist. That is how I see it, from which, however, I certainly do not conclude that everyone is a thief. But I swear there are times when I love to think so. But what's your opinion? Morality? Any psychological tricks, Charlie?"

Mr. Brown was smiling directly into Charlie's face. Mr. Brown continued: "Well, this is of course nonsense; it can't be that everybody is after something. I have never stolen anything. But you know we put a small commission for our trading services every time we sell or buy in the interest of our clients. You have never stolen anything, dear Charlie; I believe you have not. But when it comes to the point, are you ashamed to tell your story?"

## Everywhere There Is a Large Commission. There Is a High Probability of a Rip-Off

Charlie: "Perhaps the most important rule in management is to get incentive right. Worldly wisdom is mostly very, very simple. And what I am urging is not that hard to do if you have the will to plow through and do it. And the rewards are awesome—absolutely awesome. But maybe you aren't interested in awesome rewards or avoiding a lot of misery or being more able to serve everything you love in life. And, if that's your attitude, then don't pay attention to what I've been trying to tell you—because you're already on the right track.

It cannot be emphasized too much that issues of morality are deeply entwined with worldly wisdom. Considerations involving psychology. For example, take the issue of stealing.

A very significant fraction of the people in the world will steal if (a) it is very easy to do so, and (b) there's practically no chance of being caught. And once they start stealing, the consistency principle—which is a big part of human psychology—will soon combine with operant conditioning to make stealing habitual. So, if you run a business where it's easy to steal, because of your methods, you're working a great moral injury on people who work for you. Again, that's obvious. It's very, very important to create human systems that are hard to cheat. Otherwise, you're ruining your civilization because these big incentives will create incentive-caused bias, and people will rationalize that bad behavior is OK.

Then, if somebody else does it, then you've got at least two psychological principles: incentive-caused bias plus social proof. Not only that, but you get Serpico effects. If enough people are profiting in a general social climate of doing wrong, then they'll turn on you and become dangerous enemies if you try and blow the whistle. It's very dangerous to ignore these principles and let slop creep in. Powerful psychological forces are at work for evil.

How does it relate to the law business? Well, people graduate from places like Stanford Law School and go into the legislatures of our nation and, with the best motives pass laws that are easily used by people to cheat. Well, there could hardly be a worse thing you could do. Let's say you have a desire to do public service. As a natural part of your planning, you think in reverse and ask, 'What can I do to ruin our civilization?' That's easy.

If what you want to do is to ruin your civilization, just go to the legislature and pass laws that create systems wherein people can easily cheat. It will work perfectly[xlvii]."

Mr. Brown: "Well this is very interesting, but I am still more concerned with psychological case history, not an action. What really moves any individual into that? I have a very stupid and simple case. When I was a thief, I just put 30 percent over my ordinary normal fee. My client was a nut; we got a commission for my services, and I made a ton of money for him. Don't you think it is like stealing to manipulate somebody's gains? We had a dinner party on Sunday evening; recently the same risky stocks were so popular. The client was very interested to get an advantage of it. I have done it for him but charged him 30 percent over my usual fee. I took the money—nothing ashamed me at all—put it in my account, and I have no idea why. I cannot explain what happened. I felt enormous pleasure just because I got this money. I went to Las Vegas the next day and played roulette the whole night through. I drank that evening in a restaurant. I had an urge to get rid of it quickly. And it didn't trouble me, either then or later. I do not care about it right now. That's it.

"You have grown very blasé; are you ok? Maybe it is my story that… heh-heh."

Charlie: "Actually, I don't feel too well. I've got a headache, from the long day today probably."

Mr. Brown: "You need fresh country air, sir; you have to return to Omaha."

Charlie stood up, lost in his thoughts.

Mr. Brown: "In three days I'm going to have a small event with the family and some guests. How long are you going to stay in New York City? It will be a great pleasure to all of us if you managed to visit us on this occasion Sunday night."

## Have Ethics to Drive and Police Yourself

Charlie: "I will see if I will have time for it." He was thinking, "Firms should have the ethical responsibility to police themselves. Every company ought to have a long list of things that are beneath it even though they are perfectly legal. All of these money managers, frauds, mistakes, rewards, self-serving bias. Buffett and I, we don't claim to have perfect morals, but at least we have a huge area of things that are, while legal, beneath us. We won't do them. Currently, there is a culture in America that says that if it does not send you to prison, then it is ok[xlviii]."

Mr. Brown was thinking, "Charlie wants to imitate his grandfather's ideas and high standards, but who am I then? Am I born to be the total opposite of Charlie Munger? I know I have it from my father's violent passions. There is no doubt I am totally uneducated, piling up money, speculating, predicting, and following my own emotions. But I have a great mind, and I am successful. I am settled down in this house like my father. I am fond of my money. I made ten million this year. This is my passion, sitting on my moneybags, because for me passion is everything, and you make everything into passion. I started to read myself; nobody forcing me to do so, and to educate myself at the same time. Should I try to read *World Book Encyclopedia* at last? I really know nothing of the fundamentals. Maybe I will ask Charlie to give me a list of his favorite books."

They passed through the main entrance of the building in the Hamptons where Mr. Brown was living with his family; it was a great hall with numerous pictures. Mr. Brown was walking in front; Charlie followed him.

### Get Rid of Extreme Ideology. It Cabbages up the Mind

Mr. Brown: "You have to know all of these pictures were bought by my father. I have nothing to do with them. There are some favorites among them of course. Russian, Italian art, but I like especially this one." Mr. Brown pointed to a Holbein picture with the name *The Body of the Dead Christ in the Tomb*.

Mr. Brown: "Tell me, Charlie. I was planning to ask you for a long time: Do you believe in religion or ideology? I love looking inside of this picture."

Charlie: "Not drifting into extreme ideology is a very, very important thing in life. It cabbages up the mind."

Mr. Brown: "Do you have in mind young people, or is it a rule for everybody?"

Charlie: "When you're young, it's easier to drift into loyalties, and when you announce that you're a loyal member, and you start shouting the orthodox ideology out, what you're doing is pounding it in, pounding it in, and you're gradually ruining your mind. So, you want to be very, very careful of this ideology. It's a big danger[xlix]."

Mr. Brown: "I have heard Greek thinker Parmenides held the following precept: judge by rational argument. And I think there's a way to look at things rationally without falling into the trap thinking that there is no way anyone who can think honestly and clearly will always agree with me. You are absolutely correct, Charlie. Clinging to a strange ideology almost always leads to a 'cabbaged' mind. You shouldn't let ideological lies get in the way of intellectual honesty."

Charlie: "I have what I call an iron prescription that helps me keep sane when I naturally drift toward preferring one ideology over another, and that is, I saw that I'm not entitled to have an opinion on this subject unless I can state the arguments against my position better than the people who support it. I think only when I've reached that state I am qualified to speak[l]."

Charlie caught himself on a thought that over the three days in New York City, there were so many long discussions, often controversial, even about intellectual topics and mistakes, but Mr. Brown definitely took great pleasure in it. He was arguing on some matters, sometimes agreeing; it seemed he would like to know Charlie's opinion on everything.

Mr. Brown: "I understand your skepticism about overly ideological people. But is there an ideological component to what you do? Is there something that you are passionate about?"

## Charlie: Yes, I Am Passionate about Wisdom

Charlie: "Yeah. I am passionate about wisdom. I am passionate about accuracy and some kind of curiosity. Perhaps I have some streak of generosity in my nature and a desire to save values that transcend my brief life. But maybe I am just here to show off. Who knows? I believe in the discipline of mastering the best people have ever figured out. I don't believe in just sitting down and trying to dream it all up yourself. Nobody is that smart[li]."

Mr. Brown: "Do you have an explanation for practical experience over ideological ideas and people? Why are people doing that?" he said softly.

### God's Work Is Not Working. Stay Rational

Charlie: "Yes I recently had an instructive experience. I just returned from Hong Kong. I have a pal there who's a headmaster at one of the leading schools. He gave me this book called *The Language Instinct*, written by Steven Pinker. Well Pinker is a semanticist professor who rose in the shadow of Noam Chomsky—Linguistics Institute professor at MIT—who is probably the greatest semanticist who ever lived. Pinker says that human language ability is not just learned; it's deeply buried, to a considerable extent, in the genome. It is not in the genome of the animals, including the chimpanzee, to any really useful extent. It's a gift that came to humans. Pinker proves his point very well. Of course, Chomsky's already proven it. You have to be pretty ignorant not to realize that a good deal of language ability is right there in the human genome. Even though you have to work like hell to improve it through education, you start with a big leg up in your genes.

"Pinker can't understand why Chomsky—who, again, is such a genius—takes the position that the jury's still out about why this ability is in the human genome. Pinker in effect says: 'Like hell the jury is still out! The language instinct got into humans in exactly the same way that everything else got there—through Darwin's natural selection.' Well, the junior professor is clearly right—and Chomsky's hesitation is a little daft. But if a junior professor and I are right, how has a genius like Chomsky made an obvious misjudgment? The answer is quite clear to me: Chomsky is passionately ideological.

"He is an extreme egalitarian leftist who happens to be a genius. And he's so smart that he realized that if he concedes this particular Darwinian point, the implications threaten his leftist ideology. So, he naturally has his conclusion affected by his ideological bias.

"And that gets into another lesson of worldly wisdom. If ideology can screw up the head of Chomsky, imagine what it does to people like you and me. Heavy ideology is one of the most extreme distorters of human cognition. Look at these Islamic fundamentalists who just gunned down a bunch of Greek tourists shouting 'God's work[lii].'"

Mr. Brown: "You know what, dear Charlie? It seems your compassion for worldly wisdom is stronger than my compassion for everyday trading and speculation. But I often agree with you on some issues. You are in favor of objectivity and rationality. But what does it say about yourself? Your parents? Maybe your father had a strong influence on you? So, it forces you to be more objective. Where have you gotten all these principles?"

A number of paintings in old heavy gold frames adorned the walls. One full-length portrait attracted Charlie's attention. It was an old man, around sixty years old, who was wearing an army uniform with a medal around his neck.

Charlie: "That wouldn't be your father, would it?"

Mr. Brown: "That's just who it is. What about your father, Charlie?" replied Mr. Brown.

### Charlie: My Father Hated Ideology

Charlie: "There is a very interesting history if you take Warren Buffett as an example of worldly wisdom. Warren adored his father—who was a wonderful man. But Warren's father was a very heavy ideological right wing person, it happened to be, who hung around with other very heavy ideological people (right wing, naturally).

"Warren observed this as a kid. He decided that ideology was dangerous—and he was going to stay a long way away from it, which he has throughout his life. That has enormously helped the accuracy of his cognition. I learned the same lesson in a different way. My father hated ideology. Therefore, all I had to do was imitate my father and, thereby, stay on what I regard as the right path. People like Dornan on the right and Nader on the left have obviously gone a little daft. They're extreme examples of what ideology will do to you—particularly violently expressed ideology. Since it pounds ideas better than it convinces, it's a very dangerous thing to do. Therefore, in a system of multiple models across multiple disciplines, I should add as an extra rule that you should be very wary of heavy ideology. You can have heavy ideology in favor of accuracy, diligence, and objectivity. But a heavy ideology that makes you absolutely sure that the minimum wage should be raised or that it shouldn't—and it's of a holy construct where you know you're right—makes you a bit nuts.

"This is a very complicated system. Life is one damn relatedness after another. It's all right to think that, on balance, you suspect that civilization is better if the minimum wage is lowered or raised. Either position is ok. But being totally sure on issues like that with a strong, violent ideology, in my opinion, turns you into a lousy thinker. So, beware of ideology-faced mental malfunctions[liii]."

Mr. Brown: "I am still thinking of the Holbein picture, this picture. The man could lose a sense of faith if you are looking for it for a long time. It is so scary, but not you, Charlie. You happen to be not so emotionally attached to art like that." Mr. Brown went off in peals of laughter. It was strange indeed to see him laughing after looking at that picture; there was no humor in it.

Charlie was thinking this picture; Hans Holbein's painting of Christ in the tomb, such an unusual painting. The picture shows Christ, just taken from the cross. In the picture, the face is terribly sad, the eyes open. How could nature be so cruel? Anybody could lose the feeling of trust, happiness, hope, and faith. But not to him. It was definitely the right way to be this positively good man. Was it difficult? Yes, but not for him. It was difficult for the world, especially nowadays with greed and envy, and people losing their faith under pressure to make rapid decisions. There is only one positively good man, and he is Jesus Christ. This is a miracle. Charlie thinks of himself as a positively good man; the man is good but at the same time ridiculous—sometimes he finds himself ridiculously good. It seems for people he is comic and succeeds because he states the truth directly and honestly. The sympathy of this ridiculous, direct man is the secret of his success.

Mr. Brown: "I believe your opinion about ideology just beat everything else. One does not believe in God at all. Another one is so passionate about worldly wisdom. Another person could cut people's throats with a prayer. No, my dear Charlie. Truth is so strange; everybody has his own truth indeed. Ha, ha! No, that beats everything. But let's talk more about you. It is so interesting; it really is. It is enough of ideology and Christianity, concept of truth, fundamental ideas, and so forth. I would like to know actually, could you talk about why you left the law?"

Charlie: "I had a huge family. Nancy and I supported eight children. I didn't realize that the law was going to get as prosperous as it suddenly got. The big money came into law shortly after I left it. By 1962, I was mostly out. And I was totally out by 1965. So that was a long time ago. I preferred making the decisions and gambling my own money. I usually thought I knew better than the client anyway, so why should I have to do it his way? So partly, it was having an opinionated personality. And partly, it was a desire to get resources permitting independence. Also, the bulk of my clients were terrific. But there were one or two I didn't enjoy. Plus, I like the independence of a capitalist. And I'd always had sort of a gambling personality. I like figuring things out and making bets. So I simply did what came natural[liv]."

## Charlie: Warren Talked Me into Leaving the Law Business

Charlie: "Warren talked me into leaving the law business, and that was a very significant influence on me. I was already thinking about becoming a full-time investor, and Warren told me I was far better suited to that. He was right. I would probably have done it myself, but he pushed me to it. I have to say, it isn't an easy thing to work very hard for many years to build up a significant career, as I had done, and then to destroy that career on purpose."

"That would have been a lot harder to do if not for Warren's influence on me. It wasn't a mistake [laughter]. It worked out remarkably well for both of us and for a lot of other people as well [the investors in Berkshire][iv]."

Mr. Brown: "I understand you, somehow, have so many children; it has to be a great family. The days on Wall Street are hard, from time to time; you could easily go broke with all that noise around. Once I had been under total pressure, but when I was back home from work, I met my wife; she was at that time very young and pleasant with a newborn baby son. And I was so glad to look at them that I forgot all of my problems. When the baby was about six weeks, he was smiling at me for the first time. You know when they do it for the first time; it feels like something from God I see on this baby's face. So naive and forgiving. It has nothing to do with religion or feeling, just that clarity to calm me down."

After that he continued, "You know, dear Charlie, I am not the only one who wants to speak with you, by the way. Some of today's dinner guests would like to meet you as well. But there's one thing I want to tell you: don't judge them so seriously. One of my friends from childhood, he is so impulsive and not an easy person to handle. I am not sure if you will like him; he came here to meet you as well. Peter was an engineer and now started to work in money management as well; he was working on some famous construction in New York City in his early years.

The door was opened, and a young man came into the room. Mr. Brown welcomed him and introduced him to Charlie.

Peter: "Surprised, I am very surprised: I couldn't believe I'm meeting Charlie Munger in person. I have heard a lot about you—very much indeed about your famous work on the Psychology of Misjudgment. When I read it for the first time, I couldn't stop at all, then I read it another time, then repeatedly for almost one month. I heard it a hundred times as an audiobook in my car. Excellent: your collection of wisdom, mental models, and, admirably, the fact that you did it while being so busy."

Peter asked Charlie, "Why have you done it? Any motivation?"

## Avoid Casinos and Never Gamble

Charlie "To avoid being misled by the mere association of some facts with past success, use this memory clue. Think of Napoleon and Hitler when they invaded Russia after using their armies with much success elsewhere. There are plenty of mundane examples of results like those of Napoleon and Hitler. For instance, a man foolishly gambles in a casino and yet wins. This unlikely correlation causes him to try the casino again and again, and he wins more. This unlikely correlation causes him to try the casino again, and again, and again to his horrid detriment. Or a man gets lucky in some odds against a venture headed by an untalented friend. So influenced, he tries again what worked before with terrible results. The proper antidotes to being made such a patsy by past success are (1) to carefully examine each past success, looking for accidental, non-causative factors associated with what success that will tend to mislead as one appraises odds implicit in a proposed new undertaking, and (2) to look for dangerous aspects of the new undertaking that were not present when past success occurred[lvi]".

Peter: "Anyway it is very unusual for high society folks to be interested in literature and psychology. Ask Mr. Brown; it's much more fun to read news on financial blogs."

Charlie listened very carefully to what Peter had to say. He was for a moment surprised with the excellent manners of the young man, but he had to play kind, like a teacher, again. Just a waste of my time again; it is time to move away from here, Charlie was thinking.

Peter: "But you are mistaken if you think I am not successful, I am maybe not as excellent as you. I consider myself as well informed, a man of action, not as straightforward as you do—more indirect. I might not be as polite, and I have myself made many mistakes. I am not so perfectly dressed. Peter's face displayed irony, even self-pity and envy; he spoke with emotion, sometimes being unable to finish his long sentences, losing control of himself. "And yes, I am totally the opposite of you. I like to overspend my income. So what?"

Mr. Brown interrupted Peter: "Look, Peter, don't be aggressive toward Charlie. You envy him, right? Is envy good, Charlie? Don't you think it stimulates you? You work harder. What about self-serving bias, Charlie?"

**Envy Is a Way Nowhere—One of the Deadly Sins to Break You**

Charlie: "Another thing that often causes folly and ruin is the 'self-serving bias,' often subconscious, to which we're all subject. You think that 'the true little me' is entitled to do what it wants to do. And, for instance, why shouldn't the true little me get what it wants by overspending its income. Well, there once was a man who became the most famous composer in the world. But he was utterly miserable most of the time. And one of the reasons was that he always overspent his income. That was Mozart. If Mozart couldn't get by with this kind of asinine conduct, I don't think you should try it.

"By the way, the idea that caring that someone is making money faster (than you are) is one of the deadly sins. Envy is a really stupid sin because it's the only one you could never possibly have any fun at. There is a lot of pain and no fun. Why would you want to get on that trolley[lvii]?"

Peter: "Well that is fantastic, nobility and justice. All is with you and for you, Charlie Munger. But a strange thing happened: all of the capitalistic progress happens when people want to compete with each other. This is an endless process. Of course, you may disagree, but envy, especially greed, is so motivating. It must be admitted you have a great fortune in meeting Warren Buffett. Of course, he is lucky as well. But…some folks just have luck! Judge for yourself; you are still sitting in your law office. Munger, all of these litigations, for corporate people, the folks you don't really like—you have this pressure, and you don't have any time or less time for your 'thinking and reading' Do you understand how to get a billion from a legal practice? Heh-heh, I do not. I will even have to look in a dictionary for the word envy; the legend is so fresh but hard to credit. Is it any bad in envy? "

Charlie: "Envy, of course, joins chemicals in terms of causing misery. It was wreaking havoc long before it got a bad press in the laws of Moses. If you wish to retain the contribution of envy to misery, I recommend that you never read any of the biographies of that good Christian Samuel Johnson, because his life demonstrates in an enticing way the possibility and advantage of transcending envy. Resentment has always worked with me exactly as it worked for Carson. I cannot recommend it rightly enough to you if you desire misery. Johnson spoke well when he said that life is hard enough to swallow without squeezing in the bitter rind of resentment.

"For those of you who want misery, I also recommend refraining from practice of the Disraeli compromise, designed for people who find it impossible to quit resentment cold turkey. Disraeli, as he rose to become one of the greatest prime ministers, learned to give up vengeance as a motivation for action, but he did retain some outlet for resentment by putting the names of people who wronged him on pieces of paper in a drawer. Then from time to time, he reviewed these names and took pleasure in noting the way the world had taken his enemies down without his assistance[lviii]."

Peter: "But don't you think that a real misery comes from sitting and reading and a lazy life when people are like parasites—they spend their life lazy, with all of these books around. In our days, one could buy even intelligence for money, like at a marketplace. You just happened to be in the right place at the right time to buy all of these blue chips, which were undervalued. There is nothing noble in that, and now you got extraordinary results. And all of these folks who worship you on every Berkshire annual meeting gathered round a holy God that couldn't be better: intelligent, a billionaire, rational, worldy wisdom, expert on human misjudgment—all qualities at once, not something you can find in everyday life." Peter seemed to be proud when he made that statement. He was an impulsive man, but today is a day when he pointed out just everything that was in his mind. When Peter had finished, he quickly looked into Charlie's eyes. Charlie was staring back. There was nothing emotional or disappointing in Charlie's face. One could even notice that Charlie was almost expecting this kind of dialogue. Peter, without saying a word, brushed his face with his hands; he was ashamed, clearly displeased with his own statements.

Charlie was not in a position to take it personally. His thoughts were on what causes envy in economics, and one very funny story came to mind.

## Avoid Envy; Stay Unemotional and Disciplined

Charlie continued: "Dear gentlemen, let me tell you some facts on physics envy. It reminds me of a very funny Einstein story as well. The third weakness that I find in economics is what I call physics envy. And of course, that term has been borrowed from penis envy as described by one of the world's great idiots, Sigmund Freud. But he was very popular in his time, and the concept received a wide vogue.

"One of the worst examples of what physics envy did to economics was cause adoption of hard-form efficient market theory. And then, when you logically derived consequences from this wrong theory, you would get conclusions such as it can never be correct for any corporation to buy its own stock. Because the stock price, by definition, is totally efficient, there could never be any advantage. And they taught this theory to some portion of McKinsey when he was at some school of business that had adopted this crazy line of reasoning from economics, and the performer became a paid consultant for the *Washington Post*. And the *Washington Post* stock was selling at a fifth of what an orangutan could figure was the plain value per share by just counting up the values and dividing. But he so believed what he'd been taught in graduate school that he told the *Washington Post* it shouldn't buy their own stock. Well, fortunately, they put Warren Buffett on the board, and he convinced them to buy back more than half of the outstanding stock, which enriched the remaining shareholders by much more than a billion dollars. So there was at least one instance of a place that quickly killed a wrong academic theory. It's my view that economics could avoid a lot of this trouble that comes from physics envy. I want economics to pick up the basic ethos of hard science, to full attribution habit, but not the craving for an unattainable precision that comes from physics envy. The sort of precise, reliable formula that includes Boltzmann's constant is not going to happen, by and large, in economics. Economics involves too complex a system. And the craving for that physics-style precision does little but get you in trouble, like the poor fool from McKinsey.

"I think that economists would be much better off if they paid more attention to Einstein and Sharon Stone. Well, Einstein is easy because

Einstein is famous for saying, 'everything should be made as simple as possible, but no simpler.' Now, the saying is a tautology, but it's very useful, and some economists—it may have been Herb Stein—had a similar tautological saying that I dearly love: 'If a thing can't go on forever, it will eventually stop.' Sharon Stone contributed to the subject because someone once asked her if she was bothered by penis envy. And she said, 'Absolutely not. I have more trouble than I can handle with what I've got.'" Charlie alone was laughing.

After a while he continued: "Well you told me earlier today you have been so enthusiastic about psychology logical tendencies, and you heard of them at least a hundred times? Shameful reality that you couldn't put it to practice, right? Have you ever heard of lollapalooza tendency—the tendency to get extreme consequences from confluences of psychological tendencies acting in favor of a particular outcome? Psychological denial? Envy/jealousy tendency[lix]?"

Peter: "But actually if envy is so wrong, how or what is a better way to motivate people who are below the executive level to do a better job getting quality business as opposed to high volume? People like me?"

Charlie: "The young people are going to adapt to whatever the ethos is that suffocates the place. If you've got a Stanley O'Neal at the top that has to win, the ethos is going to be terrible. The ethos of the place has to change for the behavior of the place [to] change down through the chain of command. By the way, you said it was greed that has caused all this, I think you've used a wrong word: it's envy. Envy is the great driver. One investment bank can't stand the next investment bank being bigger and better. Even though the guy is making $5 million a year, he can't stand it. It's envy, and envy was in the laws of Moses. You couldn't even covet your neighbor's donkey. I mean those old Jews really knew it would cause a lot of trouble even among sheep herders. So you put it in the whole financial system and make it sacred and feed it so you have an envy-driven miasma—well, of course it's going to be a hell of a mess. The way to avoid envy to some extent was described by Aristotle. He said, 'People will adjust better if the perceived differences in outcome in society are perceived as just.' Therefore, everybody that wants to help society be stable should have a duty to arrange everything, including his own compensation, [to] be perceived elsewhere as just. Well, all I can say is that if Aristotle were still alive, he'd be a grumpy old man because his message hasn't fully been assimilated yet[ix]."

Mr. Brown: "I agree with Charlie on this matter. I suppose I have read one funny article on Warren Buffett, where Buffett said, 'Charlie kept reminding me that I was slipping into the Stone Age again. He has given me a lot more advice than I have given him. He lives a very rational life. I've never heard him say a word that expressed envy of anyone.' And you reply, 'There is an old saying: "What good is envy? It's the one sin you can't have any fun at."'"

Peter: "All people couldn't be like you, Charlie, or are we all terrible naive? How could one get a billion dollars so simply just by making the right decision? I presume this is undeserved wealth. I didn't even want to relate to you personally. I don't want to name names: I am speaking in a general sense because this wealth is undeserved. How is it possible I am working both day and night, and somebody has just bought some piece of paper?!"

Charlie: "Equality has one effect: people will literate different outcomes, if the outcomes are deserved, according to Aristotle. People are understanding that Tiger Woods is so rich. Who is getting undeserved money in America now? Not Gates or creators of businesses. Financiers are among those who receive undeserved wealth and have caused envy. Even I am guilty of this. If I said we don't want a lot of undeserved wealth, it would be extraordinary. Normal investment partnerships pay no taxes on realized gains[xi]."

## The Logic of Being Logical and Rational

Mr. Brown: "How much investment risk did you take personally once you had made enough money to live well?"

Charlie: "Most of the Munger money—I don't count the *Daily Journal*; it's just a little asterisk (laughter)—is in Berkshire Hathaway, Costco, and an Asian fund. Now, you could go to the rest of finance—they think they know how to handle money—and they'd say it's totally unthinkable, Munger doesn't know what the hell he's doing. Doesn't fit our morals. But I'm right and they're wrong. You are shrewd enough to choose well; three holdings—only one of which would support your family in perpetuity—is enough security. What difference does it make if somebody else in some year goes up 10 percent and you go down 5 percent, when you've got a thousand firms more than you need anyway? The people who make these crazy decisions don't actually have envy: what they have is clients who will fire them if they don't get the same results as everybody else. That is a crazy system. Everybody gets on the same merry-go-round. I never had any interest. As I sit here, all my securities are making new highs every day. Am I doing it wrong[lxii]?"

### Buffett: It Is Not Greed That Drives the World; It Is Envy

Peter seated himself. He noticed that for the last hour or so, he was extremely nervous, loud, and almost inpatient while Charlie was speaking. All his efforts were without any success at all; there were not any emotions on Charlie's face. Peter almost regretted some of his words. Maybe if he would learn to behave more patiently and be diligent, he would put it into habit and would be less offensive. However, the reality for him was too painful to bear—so complex, so unfair to him.

Charlie again spoke: "A member of a species designed through evolutionary process to score food is going to be driven strongly forward in getting food when it first sees food. And this is going to occur often and tend to create some conflict when the food is seen in the possession of another member of the same species. This is probably the evolutionary origin of the envy/jealousy tendency that lies so deep in human nature. And envy/jealousy is also extreme in modern life. For instance, university communities often go bananas when some university employee in money management, or some professor in surgery, receives annual compensation in multiples of the standard professional salary. And in modern investment banks, law firms, etc., the envy/jealousy effects are usually more extreme than they are in university faculties. Many big law firms, fearing disorder from envy/jealousy, have long treated all senior partners alike in compensation, no matter how different their contributions to firm welfare. As I have shared the observation of life with Warren Buffett over decades, I have heard him wisely say on several occasions: 'It is not greed that drives the world, but envy[lxiii].'"

When Charlie was finished speaking, both men had very different faces. Mr. Brown was thinking deeply; Peter was indifferent. His face indicated nothing. This man could say anything, but there was no reason to trust him or believe him.

Mr. Brown: "Charlie, don't you think that you 'have a war with yourself'? Don't you think there is unforgettable contrast between what you believe and what is actually going on in the business world right now? I appreciate you have a spiritual search for wisdom. Your image from time to time reminds me of Jesus Christ, arguing with Satan, denying God himself in this for the truth. Such confidence is a rare quality in our days. A man in whom the truth is open is a fascinating character. I really would want to copy some of your ideas, but you could be also very different. You often speak so bravely. I remember a story when you offended some people through your blind statement, but you have this human spirit and many people love you a lot. Well they do have a lot of sympathy for you. That is why they are coming to all the Berkshire events. They follow you during the *Daily Journal* Corporation meetings throughout the years. You are intellectual and idealist but very practical. You are a pure genius, Charlie.

"At the same time as you are a true capitalist, I feel you have this human suffering. It is very interesting for me to speak to you; you and Warren Buffett have to be studied as personalities, not only as value investors, but as a human beings. So many ideas and a philosophy for coping, so much work to do. It is just a wonderful thing to deal with problems from others, to avoid making your own mistakes."

### Keep On Learning. The Real Opportunities Are Few. Bet Big When You Face It

Mr. Brown was pointing to both men. "Dear gentlemen, I read psychology books as well, so I share Charlie's opinion on it. Not all of them but mostly; well I can see now the sort he is. But I totally disagree with you on the issue of the compensation system for managers or compensation for stress at the working place, under certain conditions. Do you really want to tell me it's wrong? As I know it, these people are being compensated for stress at the working place and are not cheating by playing on the feelings of others. The stress is real."

Peter: "Do you have in mind an example of the compensation system in California? This case was being discussed in every US newspaper last month"

Mr. Brown: "Yes. But I want to know what Charlie thinks about it."

Charlie Munger: "Ok. Take the workers' compensation system in California. Stress is real. And its misery can be real. So, you want to compensate people for their stress at the work place. It seems like a noble thing to do. But the trouble with such compensation is it is practically impossible to eliminate abuse. Once you reward cheating, you get crooked lawyers, crooked doctors, crooked unions, etc. participating in referral scenes. You have a total of disastrous behavior. The behavior makes all people doing it worse as they do it. So, you were trying to help your civilization. But what you did was create enormous damage, net.

"So it's much better to let some things go uncompensated—to let life be hard—rather than to create systems that are easy to cheat. Let me give you an example: I have a friend who made an industrial product at a plant in Texas far from the border. He was in a low-margin, tough business. There was massive fraud in the workers' compensation system—to a point that his premium reached double-digit percentage of payroll. And it was not that dangerous to produce his product. It's not like he was a demolition contractor or something. So he pleaded with the union, 'You've got to stop this. There is not enough money in making this product to cover all of this fraud.'

"But by then, everyone was used to it. You can't do it anymore. Incidentally, that's Pavlovian mere association, too. When people get bad news, they hate the messenger. Therefore, it was very hard for the union representative to tell all of these people that the easy money was about to stop. That is not the way to advance as a union representative. So my friend closed his plant and moved the work to Utah among a community of believing Mormons. Well, the Mormons aren't into workers' compensation fraud—at least they aren't in my friend's plant. And guess what his workers' compensation expense is today? It's two percent of payroll—down from double digits.

"That sort of tragedy is caused by letting the slop run. You must stop the slop early. It's very hard to stop the slop and moral failure if you let it run awhile."

Peter, who had been standing watching all along, said with a laugh, "This reminds me of the celebrated defense lawyer who recently used the feelings of all these naive workers as an excuse for not being compensated. They are so naive, but the lawyer himself has a great desire to rob them with big fees." He suddenly ended his speech: "It is only natural that all these poor people who were suffering a lot should have thought of being compensated. Who on Earth in their position wouldn't have thought about it? This is so funny and amusing, both ways[lxiv]."

"Enough," declared Mr. Brown. "Stop, Peter. Stop this nonsense immediately."

Peter: "It reminds me of another story. These rich people use workers in their factories and get rich. But when a real problem comes, all of the sudden they are out. They jumped away with the words 'Goodbye, guys.' That is a proper way to behave, you think? Natural capitalism, to be applauded: What a morality! But I, I don't need to show any gratitude. I have never borrowed any money from you, have I? I do not owe these capitalists anything. So what? I am not trying to win his, Charlie Munger's, gratitude. I am not interested in pleasing him."

## Capitalism and Persistence Produces Big Payoffs

"And you, how you could adore him as well? You are mad. They are so rich; they definitely go hard on our society, in terms of use only. The poor people could suffer and what? It's madness!"

Mr. Brown: "Peter, you have you lost yourself. You've lost your senses. Are you ill? This is what capitalism is all about. I believe you are not able to force any business to be in that place. Again, that's an example of what tough capitalism is. Capitalism—the way it works. You have to read Adam Smith. He is one of the wisest people that ever came along. He clearly demonstrates the productive power of the capital system. Well, it only improves productivity. The idea is that you let other people do what they do best at and stick to what you are best at. You should work in a field that is most productive for you and not be involved in this self-pity, or how hard will your life be?

"Please sit down, dear Peter." Mr. Brown himself sat down opposite Peter.

Mr. Brown was continuing his topic of capitalism, asking Charlie, "Do you think Walmart is an excellent example of capitalism? What do you think, Charlie?"

Charlie Munger: "It's quite interesting to think about Walmart starting from a single store in Bentonville, Arkansas, against Sears, Roebuck with its name, reputation and all of its billions. How does a guy in Bentonville, Arkansas, with no money blow right by Sears, Roebuck? And he does it in his own lifetime in fact, during his own late lifetime because he was already pretty old by the time he started out with one little store. He played the chain store game harder and better than anyone else. Walton invented practically nothing. But he copied everything anybody else ever did that was smart, and he did it with more fanaticism and better employee manipulation. So he just blew right by them all. He also had a very interesting competitive strategy in the early days. He was like a prize-fighter who wanted a great record so he could be in the finals and make a big TV hit. So what did he do? He went out and fought forty-two paloo-kas. Right? And the result was knockout, knockout, knockout—forty-two times. Walton, being as shrewd as he was, basically broke other small-town merchants in the early days. With his more efficient system, he might not have been able to tackle some titan head-on at the time. But with his better system, he could destroy those small-town merchants. And he went around doing it time after time after time. Then, as he got bigger, he started destroying the big boys. Well, that was a very, very shrewd strategy[lxv]."

## Challenge Yourself. Do the Best You Can Do

Peter: "Excellently put and quite right about Walmart. In any case, what I found most astonishing, from your point, is that you are not humble enough from the point of view of humanity. You know these workers; some of them are maybe really dying, so you have no compassion because of your morals, social values, and responsibilities? These people are poor, but all you do is the beauty and elegance of reading, wisdom—it's what you live for, isn't it? I am original myself. I don't want to be around people like you…learn it…copy ideas. I am a simple man, a worker".

Charlie Munger: "Your originality is overrated. I believe in the discipline of mastering the best that other people have figured out. I don't believe in just sitting down and trying to dream it all up yourself. Nobody's that smart.

"What should we compare is not ourselves against others. We should compare who we are today against who we were yesterday, who we are today against who we will be tomorrow. This may be simple and obvious: true happiness is found in a life of constant advancement. Problems resolved with courage and wisdom can be a source of joy[lxvi]."

Peter was hardly listening to Charlie; he had no attention, nor the curiosity to listen to him any longer.

Peter: "I am very grateful that all you gentlemen have let me speak. You are people, so intelligent and with all of these numerous observations and stories. Thanks a ton for allowing me to have my point of view, which is different or worse…"

"You are absolutely right, Peter. I am sick and tired of you tonight. You'd better go home," said Mr. Brown.

"Well, goodbye!" he said in reply. He started to laugh again. "I think it rather easy to say 'good bye' to you. You are Excellency, Charlie Munger. I have a big honor tonight." He looked at everybody a little sad and angry and left the room. Mr. Brown took enormous pleasure in Peter leaving the room. He could not object to this young man having an opinion. He was a respected son of his friend, but this was just too much.

The same moment the door opened, and Charlie and Mr. Brown were invited to the main hall for the dinner. There were plenty of thoughts at that time in Mr. Brown's head: "Charlie's mind is a prepared mind, and there is not some magic investment formula, which could explain how it works. He prefers to focus intelligently on preparation of his mind".

Mr. Brown's villa was luxuriously finished. It reminded one of a Swiss chalet; very elegant flowers were everywhere, the garden beautifully decorated. The hall was made as a veranda so everybody could look outside. It was spacious. Charlie and Mr. Brown joined other guests in the hall.

Charlie noticed he was nervous; he had been extremely tired by the conversation. His attention was attracted only to things that interested him, and when he was asked a question, his face and even posture expressed self-confidence, rationality, and trust.

Mr. Brown's wife was an elegant woman, nicely dressed. Alexandra came to Charlie and Mr. Brown and was introduced to Charlie. She smiled and said, "If you allow, ladies and gentlemen, I will ask Charlie a question. I just want to satisfy my own curiosity. Dear Charlie, were you born so intelligent?" She smiled so pleasantly. "I hope you will tell me and our guests about yourself. Your personal education history?"

Charlie: "Next, my personal education history is interesting because it has deficiencies, and my peculiarities eventually created advantages. For some odd reason, I had an early and extreme multidisciplinary cast of mind. I couldn't stand reaching for a small idea in my own discipline when there was a big idea right over the fence in somebody else's discipline. So, I just grabbed in all directions for the big ideas that would really work. Nobody taught me to do that; I was just born with that yen." And: "The first rule is that you can't really know anything if you just remember isolated facts and try and bang 'em back[lxvii]."

Alexandra: "What about economics? Where have you studied it? Do you like to read intellectual books only?"

Charlie: "Adam Smith was so good a thinker and so good a writer that, in his own time, Emmanuel Kant, then the greatest intellectual in

Germany, simply announced there was nobody in Germany to equal Adam Smith. Well, Voltaire, being an even pithier speaker than Kant, immediately said, Oh well, France does not have anybody who can even be compared to Adam Smith. So economics started with some very great men and great writers. Later there have been great writers like John Maynard Keynes, whom I quote all the time and who had added a great amount of illumination to my life[xviii]."

One of Mr. Brown friends: "Dear Charlie, I recall I was reading an article by you, two or three months ago. It was about objectivity and its connection to the legal system. In addition, talented defense lawyers just have to be trained to be multidisciplinary. I was very glad you were discussing it. I was so glad to see you discussing it, as it reflects my point of view well."

## Rationality and Objectivity Will Work

Charlie thought for a while, and then spoke softly: "The standard way lawyers think is to weight both sides. There's forced objectivity and a procedural system. That's a huge plus. So if that's what you're talking about regarding law practice, but a lot of that's not good, a lot of it has drifted away. It's not at all uncommon that filling rates exhaust the amount in dispute before you get to trial. If you're doing this as a lawyer, that's a moral minefield.

"The legal profession attracts a lot of smart people who can express themselves well in words and numbers. There are many good people coming out because many good people are going in. Yet much of what law schools do is a joke. I think that rationality and objectivity will work. But what works for you may not work for others[lxix]."

Mr. Brown: "Well, but we all here, my guests, everybody knows you as a very rational person in investing. You never speculate and make any macroeconomic predictions. This is what Berkshire is famous for. But speculation is the nature of the market; it always has been, not just in this country, but everywhere, and I could imagine, will continue to take place for a long time. Of course, we all know some famous stories, so we talk openly and read about them. What do you think, Charlie?"

Charlie: "All you have to do is keep trying to learn at the temple of rationality and do things when it makes sense. I am quite prosperous even though I didn't invest in K-Mart's bankruptcy. You can miss a lot. We bought 4 percent of Freddie Mac [many years ago]. None of Fannie Mae. How could the same mind have done that?! It wasn't very smart. But despite the cognitive mistakes [we've made], we're a lot richer now than we were then. I think you need constantly to remember the mistakes of omission. We're very good at this. Nobody remembers then—nobody thinks less of me for missing K-Mart—but I think about it every day. It is a very [useful discipline to have]. Chris Davis [of Davis Advisors] who's not here, has a temple of shame for mistakes. [It's a wall in his office in which he hangs stock certificates of the worst stocks he's ever invested in.] But this is inadequate. You need a temple of shame squared—great things you almost did and had you been more rational, should have invested in. You will be a lot better investor if you do this. You ought to remember boners of both kinds. Reality doesn't distinguish—either way, in ten years, you're poorer. So why not celebrate your mistakes in both categories[lxx]?"

Mr. Brown: "Of course there are a lot of mistakes and failures in modern finance. I have visited money managers with the best reputation recently. There are even worse stories than what Charlie told. But there was one thing I noticed: the most hardened and unpleasant people are, all the same, aware that they are criminals, but there is nothing wrong with that. Denial? I don't know. There was one case when a guy acted wrongly, and he knew that it was going to be a catastrophe later, but he even wanted to acknowledge himself as a criminal. They think of themselves as very successful money managers. So that is all right. This is where the terrible difference lies, exactly here. They have in mind this is a normal way to live a life."

Charlie had started laughing by now. Alexandra was thinking, and asking her husband, "And why are you so surprised at him? And you, Charlie, do you believe in the importance of being an exemplar to lead people, to show the right behavior in finance?"

Charlie Munger: "I think people have a duty to rise high in life, to be exemplars. A guy who rises high in the army or becomes a Supreme Court justice is expected to be an exemplar, so why shouldn't a guy who rises high in a big corporation act as an exemplar and not take every last penny? It is not a problem we've had at Berkshire, but look at how far it's spread. We have about two imitators [laughter][lxxi]."

Well Alexandra was thinking, of course he meant himself and Buffett. Who else is doing that in modern money management?

"Dear Charlie," said Mr. Brown, "it is not that easy to get rid of all difficulties and to establish paradise on Earth, and you do seem to count on that a little. Honesty, ethics—using these qualities to create an ideal society is a more difficult business than it seems to you right now. I think we'd better change the subject of our discussion right now, otherwise we will all be embarrassed again by Charlie's truth."

Alexandra: "Yes, gentlemen. Is there time for a professional life learning about these mental models, and doing whatever else interests you? Do you find time to do fun things besides learning?"

**Good Behavior and Principles Are Beneficial. Stick to Them**

Charlie: "I've always taken a fair amount of time to do what I really wanted to do—some of which was merely to fish, play bridge, or play golf. Each of us must figure out his or her own lifestyle. You may want to work seventy hours a week for ten years to make partner at Grovath and thereby obtain the obligation to do more of the same. Or you may say, 'I'm not willing to pay that price.' Either way, it's a totally personal decision that you have to make by your own lights. But, whatever you decide. I think it's a huge mistake not to absorb elementary worldly wisdom if you are capable of doing it because it makes you better able to serve others; it makes you better able to serve yourself, and it makes life more fun. So, if you have aptitude for doing it, I think you'd be crazy not do. Your life will be enriched—not only financially, but in a host of other ways—if you do. I, myself, have never taken a course in psychology, but I'm telling you now that all of the psychology textbooks are wrong. This is very eccentric. But all I can tell you is that I am sincere[lxxii]."

Charlie was thinking, I never want to please all of these people. All of these people reminded him first of all of a duty, a duty to give back to society. What is the right way to do it? Well, it brings more fun and joy to speak at events at Harvard or Caltech. Charlie was demanding, demanding first for himself. He was in search of new knowledge, truth, and this has made him a much better man.

He was thinking that some women were dressed elegant while not being festive or fashionable. The music played in the background. All of these guests today, they know each other; they came together to meet each other. Many of them enjoyed the talks with pleasure. The evening was beautiful, but some folks were standing near Charlie all the time, attracted by his personality. People were always curious about Charlie; he reminded them of a computer who gave exact answers, and nobody was as correct as Charlie was. Among "the groupies," as Charlie called these people, were very outstanding and intelligent people.

The same moment Mr. Brown asked Charlie's permission to introduce him to another friend, they shook one another's hand, and the friend asked him some question, but Charlie did not reply; he was thinking about going off somewhere, just disappearing; he just wanted to be alone with his thoughts and a book, to just sit in his favorite chair and be alone, maybe day and night. He was dreaming of coming back to his family to Omaha, where he was raised, maybe to meet his old friends and relatives, whom he had not visited for a long time, to see this beautiful landscape, white clouds. Oh, how he wished he were there now. "Worldly wisdom and knowledge came to me not because I am so intelligent, but I succeed because I have a long attention span. So, I devote time constantly to looking and searching for the knowledge and wisdom. Why aren't the rest of these people just doing the same thing? It is so easy…"

Mr. Brown came to him and, interrupting his thoughts, said, "I am so upset; one of my companies is not doing very well right now, and it can even go into bankruptcy. It is a mess. I cannot go to sleep. I have come to speak to you because of our friendship; you are a very special person, an incomparable person. I mean, you do not tell lies perhaps at all. I need a friend like you, a trusted person with trusted opinions. Now I rather need to know your opinion on every subject. I highly appreciate it, Charlie. I really do. I am sure you have a lot to tell about allocation of capital, as well as, about people, your short funny stories about incentive bias are so much fun. But let's speak about basics. Financial economists in recent years have rediscovered that highly profitable, high-quality companies are better investments than other companies are. They try to figure out where this idea came from. How did you come to this idea? You were not even Charlie Munger then."

[Laughter]

### Disagreement with Yourself Is Healthy. Learn to Kill Your Most Beautiful Ideas

Charlie Munger: "Everybody with any sense at all knows that some companies are better than others. What makes it difficult is they sell at higher prices in relation to assets, and earnings and so forth, and that takes the fun out of the game. If all you had to do was figure out which companies were better than others, an idiot could make a lot of money. But they keep raising the prices to where the odds change. I always knew that. They were teaching my colleagues that the stock market was so efficient that nobody could beat it. But I knew people who beat the pari-mutuel system in Omaha by knowing more about horses than other people. I knew it was bull. When I was young I never went near a business school so I didn't get polluted by craziness [laughter].

"I never believed it. I never believed there was a talking snake in the Garden of Eden. I had a gift for recognizing twaddle, and there's nothing remarkable about it. I don't have any wonderful insights that other people don't have. I just avoided idiocy slightly more consistently than others. Other people are trying to be short, all I am trying to be is non-idiotic. I've found that's all you have to do to get not cheated in life, is to be non- idiotic and live a long time. It's harder to be non- idiotic than most people think[lxxiii]."

Mr. Brown was overexcited with Charlie's answer and added, "Get right to the point, Charlie. You want to tell me that this theory of efficient market does not exist at all? Well I, myself, have been taught at school and then at university. Sometimes I want to laugh about myself; you just destroy my theory. I really love your arguments, Charlie. I have a feeling we are in a temple, and you give me all of these intellectual stories and courses. 'Intellectual courses.' You know, I am fond of reading these Wall Street researches and comments. It influences me; I like to act. I am comfortable with its hectic pace and gambling. I understand the rules of the game. I share their opinion on many subjects. This is what is so attractive to folks like me: we are gamblers. I feel myself to be an artist—honestly, Charlie! So, what does it mean, all of this teaching is not useful at all? You want to tell me this evil is coming to earth to teach us wrong theories. But your results are amazing. But I have more fun. What is it about Berkshire's records? How have you managed to get these results?"

## Stock Market Is Not Efficient

Charlie Munger: "I watched the same thing happen at the Jules Stein Eye Institute at UCLA. I asked, at one point, Why are you treating cataracts only with a totally obsolete cataract operation? And the man said to me, 'Charlie, it's such a wonderful operation to teach.' When he stopped using this operation, it was because almost all the patients had voted with their feet. Again, appeal to interest and not to reason if you want to change conclusions.

"Well, Berkshire's record has been archived without paying one ounce of attention to the efficient market theory in its hard form. And not one ounce of attention to the descendants of that idea, which came out of academic economics and went into corporate finance and morphed into such obscenities as the capital asset pricing model, which we also paid no attention to. I think you'd have easily outperformed the marked by seven percentage points per annum just by investing in high-volatility stocks.

"Yet, believe it or not, like Jules Stein's doctor, people once believed this stuff. And the belief was rewarded. And it spread. And many people still believe it. But Berkshire never paid any attention to it. And now, I think the world is coming our way; the idea of perfection in all market outcomes is going the way of the dodo.

"It was always clear to me that stock markets couldn't be perfectly efficient, because as a teenager, I'd been to the racetrack in Omaha, where they had the pari-mutuel system. It was quite obvious to me that the house take, the croupiers' take, was 17 percent; some people consistently lost a lot less than 17 percent of all of their bets. And so, I didn't accept the argument that the stock market was always perfectly efficient in creating rational prices. Indeed, there have been documented cases of people getting so good at understanding houses and odds that they actually are able to beat the house in off-track betting. There aren't many people who can do that, but there are a few people in America who can[lxxiv]."

Mr. Brown was from time to time making a very surprised face. "If the efficient theory doesn't work as you said before, what is the model you suggest? I just want to understand you better; isn't that practical in total, sir? You are so honest and straightforward, and all of these wonderful credits and profit you have done with Buffett through the years. We couldn't ignore it. I think the people have to be interested in ideas like that, to ask the right question from the right people. I consider anyone who isn't interested in finding out the truth is just bonkers.

"Everybody is so selfish nowadays; everybody wants success in any way possible; it is a material necessity. People have no time to think for themselves; all they want is to have a lot of cash. Then they come to people like me and trust us with their money. But from time to time, I couldn't trust myself. He, he.

"You are playing poker, Charlie. Is it helping you to know the rules and to play it accordingly? Tell me, what happens in stock markets, then? A shrewd horseplayer's edge reduces the average loss. This is probably true. Again, that is not the point. This is not about humanity, Charlie. The folks need to live and eat today, don't you think? Not tomorrow. I don't have that time to wait. The point is in the following story. Have you read Darwin's *Voyage of the Beagle*? You have done it. I know you like Darwin; I definitely know you have. I feel I must read this story once again, one of my favorites. I feel myself so familiar with it, and yes, it is applicable in our time, in our country, which, Charlie, you love as I do. This story's moral is what right and wrong are just illusions of our mind. The book is right here with me; I will read it for you right now:

"I heard Mr. Law, a scaling-master intimate with the natives (Fuegians) of this country; give a curious account of a state of a party of one hundred and fifty natives on the West Coast who were very thin and in great distress…From the concurrent, but quite independent evidence of the boy taken by Mr. Law, and of Jeremy Button, it is certainly true, that when pressed in winter by hunger, they kill and devour their old women before they kill their dogs. The boy, being asked by Mr. Law why they did this, answered, "Doggies catch otters, old women no." This boy described the manner in which they were killed by being held over smoke and thus choked, he imitated their screams as a joke, and described the parts of their bodies which were considered best to eat. Horrid as such a death by the hands of their friends and relatives must be, the fears of the old women, when hunger begins to press, are more painful to think of we, were told that they then ran away into the mountains, but that they are pursued by the men and brought back to the slaughter-house at their own firesides[lxxv]"!

Mr. Brown was continuing after a short pause: "For me this is a simple, understandable concept, you know; there is no word fair or bonkers in the market. You got what you deserved, right? If this is the way that I earn this money. Moreover, it is legal; who could explain to me why I could not do it anymore? This case from Darwin shows that cannibalism is a normal process; there is not so much bad or unfair in that story. So I allow and consider myself as a hero of our time." Mr. Brown smiled.

Charlie was thinking he did not want to continue any discussion for tonight. He was simply in a good mood; he gave Mr. Brown a friendly smile. The evening was over.

Many thoughts were in Charlie's mind when he left that dinner; some of them had a philosophical meaning as he was preoccupied by both fear and failure—to be precise, not to repeat any mistakes he had already done. Moreover, the second was to believe in humanity. The success in life in his long life was achieved because he was a good man, rather than good institutions. He was thinking how hard were the times when his young son was dying in his arms (the death of his son Teddy happened when the boy was only nine years old), and divorce from his first wife. It was horrible—absolutely horrible. But one has to go through life without the feelings of self-pity and resentment. Man has an obligation to stay humble, stay rational. Yet Charlie was losing his eyesight, which is a tragedy for a man who loves to read. And it was also worst during the last months. It was painful; he was concerned not to think about it. Charlie, as always, was idolizing Benjamin Franklin in his thoughts. This emulation to improve, to constantly search for improvement, is one of the characteristics of his personality. Charlie worked indeed very hard on that; it wasn't possible all the time. Franklin wrote, "For, even if I could conceive that I had completely overcome [my pride], I should probably be proud of my humility[lxxvi]." Charlie was thinking the same: "In my whole life, nobody accused me of being humble. Although humility is a trait I much admire, I don't think I got my full share[lxxvii]." He defines this characteristic as being key for his success. Charlie was constantly thinking why other people are not copying and incorporating these principles, which are so logical. It is so essential, constantly searching and learning and constantly applying his mental models approach to solve life's problems apart from investing—it is only the right way.

What most people want is, was, and will be only to acquire more money, wealth, and power. But the most important thing is to copy ideas, to find the right heroes, then to make a combination of a genius and a fanatic to acquire the logic of wisdom when one is young enough to have a long run. Human mental limitations not everybody takes seriously. Our natural weaknesses: we have confirmation bias; we pick out evidence that supports our views, we are cognitive misers; we try to think as little as possible; we are hard thinkers and conform our perceptions to fit in with the group.

Should the spiritual values of a good man dominate over the material? The correct answer is yes. Contemporary materialism is killing many men. It is so important to have a sincerity in the things you are doing every day. Think innocently and justly, and if you speak, speak accordingly.

Have humility in emulating Benjamin Franklin; imitate Jesus and Socrates. This is a portrait of a positively good man. Sometimes he was thinking that the whole world and contemporary America, Wall Street were paralyzed with the evils of egoism, bad ethics, self-interest, and personal wealth. Materialism is a good thing when it is not seduced by the power of finance. Wall Street is the best example of evil, ever.

Richard Dawkins said, "In a universe of electrons and selfish genes, blind physical forces and genetic replication, some people are going to get hurt, other people are going to get lucky, and you won't find any rhyme or reason in it, nor any justice. The universe that we observe has precisely the properties we should expect, at the bottom, no design, no purpose, no evil and no greed, nothing but pitiless indifference. As that unhappy poet A.E. Houseman put it: 'For nature, heartless, witless nature, will neither care nor know'—DNA neither cares nor knows. DNA just is and we dance to its music.

"A universe with a God would look quite different from a universe without one. A physics, a biology where there is God is bound to look different so the most basic claims of religion are scientific[lxxviii]."

These thoughts finally raised him to such different conclusions. He was tired today; enough of thinking. What he wanted right now was to hurry up, to speak with Warren on the phone and then to sleep and be done with it all. It was silent; Charlie was in his bed in his room at the hotel and fell asleep.

Charlie spent a few more days in New York City. Although he blamed himself for the meetings with Mr. Brown and his friends, he was quite happy to meet him again. Sometimes he had been blaming himself for speaking the truth, but at the same time, he was not able to change. He was thinking of this young fellow Peter; he was kind of naïve and young but not stupid. Mr. Brown mentioned yesterday he would invite Peter to their meeting as well. Peter attacked capitalism not because he was naïve. He attacked Charlie in person because he didn't have money himself. This was like a modern apocalypse, the way Peter was thinking about life.

Charlie reminded himself of a speech from 1998: "To conclude, I will make one controversial prediction and one controversial argument. The controversial prediction is that, if some of you make your investment style more like Berkshire Hathaway's, in a long-term retrospect, you will be unlikely to have cause for regret, even if you can't get Warren Buffet to work for nothing. Instead, Berkshire will have cause for regret as it faces more intelligent investment competition. But Berkshire won't actually regret any disadvantage from your enlightenment. We only want what success we can get despite encouraging others to share our general views about reality. My controversial argument is an additional consideration weighing against the complex high cost investment modalities becoming ever more popular at foundations. Even if, contrary to my suspicions, such modalities should turn out pretty well, most of the money-making activities would contain profoundly antisocial effects. This would be so because the activity would exacerbate the current, harmful trend in which ever more of the nation's ethical young brainpower is attracted into lucrative money management and its attendant modern frictions, as distinguished from work providing much more value to others. Money management does not create the right examples. Early Charlie Munger is a horrible career model for the young because not enough was delivered from capitalism and other similar career models are even worse. Rather than encourage such models, a more constructive choice of foundations is long-term investment concentration in a few domestic corporations that are widely admired. Why not just imitate Ben Franklin? After all, old Ben was very effective in doing public good. And he was a pretty good investor too. Better his model, I think, then Bernie Cornfield's. The choice is plainly yours to make[lxxix]."

However, there were some money managers who have won Charlie's respect. First of all Charlie was thinking about Ted Combs. Ted Combs was from Australia and was going to meet Charlie. Ted was not sure he would get that meeting. However, to his surprise, they met, and afterward Ted got to meet with Warren as well. Ted is a nice and intelligent person, a young one too. They put him in charge of Berkshire Hathaway acquisition. Another one was his longtime friend and investor Mohnish Pabrai[1]. Like Buffett, Pabrai looks at stocks not as piece of paper but as ownership of a business. He has no interest in a company that looks 10 percent undervalued. If he does not think the opportunity is blindingly obvious, he passes. The most important quality is his patience; this is a rare gift, Charlie thought.

---

[1] https://en.wikipedia.org/wiki/Mohnish_Pabrai

Most money managers are crazy. They spend their time multitasking, jumping around emails, and following the noise of the crowd around them. They all have an obsession about beating the market. These are totally very different personalities from Warren and Charlie. Charlie lives a very rational life. If you keep learning all the time, you have a wonderful advantage. The only way to make really big money over time is to invest in a good business and stick with it for a long time.

### Rudyard Kipling's Poem "If"[Lxxx]

Definitely one of the best money managers on this planet is Warren Buffett. Charlie has no doubt about it. On his way to the busy meeting, he remembered Rudyard Kipling's poem:

> If you can keep your head when all about you.
> Are losing theirs and blaming it on you.
> If you can trust yourself when all men doubt you.
> But make allowance for their doubting too;

> If you can wait and not be tired of waiting,
> Or being lied about, don't deal in lies,
> Or being hated, don't give way to hating,
> And yet don't look too good, not talk too wise;

> If you can dream—and not make dream your master;
> You can think—and not make thoughts your aim;
> If you can meet with triumph and disaster,
> And treat those two imposters just the same;
> If you can bear to hear the truth you've spoken,
> Twisted by knaves to make a trap for fools,
> Or watch the things you gave your life to broken…

> And—which is more—you'll be a Man, my son!

The same time, in another part of New York City, in his apartment, Peter was thinking: "Yesterday evening Charlie came to visit Mr. Brown and of course he is invited today as well. Among other things, Charlie tried to persuade me of his way of thinking. I know he will be talking with me the same way today; he is so straight about these things. It seems his decision-making process and not all of this complicated stuff is applicable to me. He is materialistic. As he never lies, he finds himself so significant. I have to study him carefully. I do not know whether I like him or not. I have no time for these considerations now. Who knows why then I am coming to meet him again for lunch, but I have to anticipate. I am not lying anyway; I always say nothing but the truth. We are just different people, he and I. He is materialistic, but I need such a man who would finally tell me a naked truth, without any pleasure to be loved or liked; he has this straightforwardness and my respect.

"If I talk to him like 'I'm poor, a miserable person. I work like a horse. My wife divorced me. I am hungry. I cannot afford to buy medicine. My eldest daughter was given to a parenting house because we couldn't raise her at home, as we had not enough money to raise her. I was so young.' If I just complain, will I win any sympathy in his eyes? Others do not have to work, and read all the time and wear expensive clothes and beautiful homes, yet they are rich! And he will probably answer, 'I never had any pity for these fools, never.' Why I was born not to be Charlie Munger himself? Whose fault is it that I do not have his billions? I am indeed his opposite reflection. Maybe I was born to be the opposite of Charlie Munger. He is old, and he thinks he knows everything. If he is alive, everything must be within his power!

"Am I taking this life too lightly, too cheaply, too lazily? I am quite happy about myself. Christopher Columbus also discovered America without knowing about it, and he was happy to make all of these discoveries. Columbus died without knowing that he discovered the New World. What matters is this discovery. And at this lunch today I again will sit down with him, feeling like I am in a morality and ethics school. This gets on my nerves. Why am I going there today to hear his stories about humility? I will probably laugh from time to time. But I will go. You know why: because he is so direct and straightforward and he doesn't suffer fools at all. He will of course tell me that my poverty is due to a lack of discipline and patience and I deserve it. And I will tell him that I read a story in today's newspaper where some good parents 'frozen the baby to death,' and I will ask if the baby deserved it. Whose fault was that? Or the parents of a young guy who was dying from a strange disease, so they have to put him to a special hospital to take care but they don't have any money for the treatment." Everything was mixed in Peter's head right now; he was definitely angry.

The lunch had been organized by Mr. Brown at his house. It was a champagne lunch. It was very nice weather this day when Peter came to Mr. Brown's house; both he and Charlie were already there. Peter was asked if he preferred the wine or the champagne. He took champagne. He wanted to be a little drunk. Mr. Brown was talking about delight and thanked Charlie for something. How happy he was to be around a best friend. He was thanking Charlie for the charity evening that he had organized before and said that people do think wrong, but that individual efforts and acts of charity were very important. Peter had anticipated the conversation from the beginning. You could see it in his face; he did not share the ideas of Mr. Brown.

## Life Is Unfair. Move On

Peter: "Dear Charlie, dear Mr. Brown, you know I am not as moral as you guys, but can you explain to me one thing? Some of my friends—you don't know them—they helped a prisoner out of a jail because they wanted to be so noble to help that 'unfortunate,' who maybe killed several people before, just for the fun of it without any reason. You can be sure such kind of people exist in our society. How can you know what is the right way to deal with such people, murderers for example? And if you really helped them with your nice words? Nevertheless, this is a very noble thing to do, very well. I am not denying it, but the most significant role is that your good behavior will be copied, so it will not be forgotten. It will pass from one to another." After a short pause, Peter continued: "And how one can stand up after the worst falls in one's life? How and what do you think, Charlie?" Charlie turned his head.

Charlie: "My prescription for misery is to go down and stay down when you get your first, second, and third severe reverse in the battle of life. Because there is so much adversity out there, even for the lucky and wise this will guarantee that in due course you will be permanently mixed in misery. Ignore at all cost the lesson contained in the accurate epitaph written for himself by Epictetus: 'Here lies Epictetus, a slave, maimed in body, the ultimate in poverty and favored by the Gods[lxxxi].'

"Another thing to cope with is that life is very likely to provide terrible blows, unfair blows. Some people recover, and others don't. And there I think the attitude of Epictetus helps guide one to the right reaction. He thought that every mischance, in life, however bad, created an opportunity to behave well. He believed every mischance provided an opportunity to learn something useful. And one's duty was not to become immersed in self-pity, but utilize each terrible blow in a constructive fashion. His ideas were very sound, influencing the best of the Roman Empire—Marcus Aurelius and many others—over many centuries[lxxxii]."

Peter: "No, Charlie, just think for a moment. Let us say practically that you, for example, has lost your job and have three children and a wife at home, and you only have three months to live. Could you still be a positive, good man doing good deeds? An amusing thought, you must admit, Charlie."

Mr. Brown was thinking what a shame it was to speak with this Peter; he had stubborn abilities to turn everyone in his dialogue to opposition. He was always correct—only he was always right. Stupidity! As this young man was probably in need of treatment, he clearly denied every argument of another side. Mr. Brown wanted to apologize to Charlie for Peter's misbehavior. He would like even to tell this young poor fellow he was full of envy, a greedy, impatient nobody. However, he did not. For a moment, he saw Charlie's face. It was not a big surprise for Charlie to see young people speaking this way. Mr. Brown decided to change the topic of discussion or to have it in a more "productive way." He rather hated this direct opposition, the angry faces and stubbornness. He felt he belonged to the best intellectual circle to speak the truth indirectly.

## Winner Work on Avoiding Psychological Denial

Mr. Brown: "You know, dear Charlie, people are very different. You know it very well indeed; you have been very engaged with psychology for a long time. There is a big difference between patience and stubbornness. Patience is the willingness to wait a long time while remaining open to changing your mind when the facts change. Stubbornness is the willingness to wait a long time while ignoring and dismissing evidence that you are wrong. Just some people, they are your guests. I remember the tendency from your work on the Psychology of Human Misjudgment about pain-avoiding psychology denial. Could you be so kind to tell us more about it? Our young friend may be in need of some practical stories." Mr. Brown was smiling at Peter.

Charlie: "This phenomenon first hit me hard in World War II when the superathlete, superstudent son of a family friend flew off over the Atlantic Ocean and never came back. His mother, who was a very sane woman, then refused to believe he was dead. That's simple, pain-avoiding psychological denial. The reality is too painful to bear, so one distorts the facts till they become bearable. We all do that to some extent, often causing terrible problems. The most extreme outcomes are usually mixed up with love, death, and chemical dependency.

"Where denial is used to make dying easier, the conduct meets almost no criticism. Who would begrudge a fellow man such help at such a time? But some people hope to love life holding to the iron prescription 'It is not necessary to hope in order to persevere.' And there is something admirable in anyone able to do this. In chemical dependency, wherein morals usually break down horribly, addicted persons tend to believe that they remain in respectable condition, with respectable prospects. They then display an unrealistic denial of reality as they go deeper into deterioration. In my youth, Freudian remedies failed utterly in reversing chemical dependency, but nowadays Alcoholics Anonymous routinely achieves a 50 percent cure rate by causing several psychological tendencies to work together to counter addiction. However, the cure process is typically difficult and draining, and a 50 percent success rate implies a 50 percent fail rate. One should stay far away from any conduct at all likely to drift into chemical dependency. Even a small chance of suffering so great a damage should be avoided[lxxxiii]."

Peter: "Yes, but I mean…how shall I put it? Berkshire Hathaway, and I am sure you as well, made a lot mistakes. Do you want to tell me that you acknowledge all of them together?! I heard Warren Buffett has said that the investment Berkshire made in an airline was a good example of what not to do. What chain of thinking led to that wrong conclusion?"

**It Is Better to Fix Your Mistakes Faster Than You Can Make Them**
Charlie: "We were not buying stock in USAir on the theory that the common shareholders were certain to prosper—because the history of the airline business in terms of taking care of shareholders had been terrible. It was a preferred stock with a mandatory redemption. In effect, we were loaning money to USAir, and we had this equity kicker.

"We were not guessing whether it would be a great place for the shareholders. We were guessing whether it would remain prosperous enough to pay off the credit for the investment—carrying a fixed dividend and a mandatory redemption. We guessed that the business would not get so bad that we'd have a credit threat for which we were not being adequately compensated by the high rate we were getting. As it happened, USAir went right to the brink of going broke. It was hanging by a thread for several months. It's since come back. And we'll probably get all our money back plus the whole coupon. But it was a mistake. I don't want you to think we have any way of learning or behaving so you won't make a lot of mistakes. I am just saying that you can learn to make fewer mistakes than other people—and how to fix your mistakes faster when you do make them. But there is no way that you can live an adequate life without (making) many mistakes. Failure to handle psychological denial is a common way for people to go broke. You've made an enormous commitment to something. You've poured effort and money in. And the more you put in, the more that the whole consistency principle makes you think, 'Now it has to work, if I put just a little more then it'll work.'"

## Benjamin Franklin. When in Doubts Don't

"And deprival super-reaction syndrome comes in: you are going to lose the whole thing if you don't put in a little more. People go broke that way—because they can't stop, rethink and say, 'I can afford to write this one off and live to fight again. I don't have to pursue this thing as an obsession—in a way that will break me[lxxxiv].'"

Peter: "Well, that is very interesting, your thought about denial. But don't you think a part of investing is that over optimism is a huge problem as well. Do they connect one to another?"

Charlie: "About three centuries before the birth of Christ, Demosthenes, the most famous Greek orator, said, 'What a man wishes that also he believes.' Demosthenes, parsed out, was thus saying that man displays not only simple pain-avoiding psychological denial but also an excess of optimism even when he is already doing well.

"The Greek orator was clearly right about an excess of optimism being the normal human condition, even when pain or the threat of pain is absent. Witness happy people buying lottery tickets or believing that credit-furnishing, delivery-making grocery stores were going to displace a great many superefficient cash-and-carry supermarkets. One standard antidote to foolish optimism is trained, habitual use of the simple probability math of Fermat and Pascal, taught in my youth to high school sophomores. The mental rules of thumb that evolution will deal with risk are not adequate. They resemble the dysfunctional golf grip you would have if you relied on a grip driven by evolution instead of golf lessons[lxxxv]."

Peter: "Well, all right, all right, Charlie; this is really interesting. I see I used a very stupid expression when I called you a total materialist. I just did it…to test you. As it seems now you are a big expert on human psychology. Treat it please as if it were never said. If I happened to offend you, please forgive me. Sometimes I myself am afraid of what I said to others. I have read very passionately your speech on 'The Psychology of Human Misjudgment,' and you know what my favorite part is? It is the part where you described these dogs under stress conditions. So all people, traders, who are working under stress conditions are like a dogs? Moreover, this is a very correct idea. This is indeed a brilliant one. I feel so much pressure working on Wall Street. You know it, and I am used to that. There is so much stress. We receive these calls from angry clients; the world is going to hell. I don't realize whether it is night or day, and who cares? But at a certain point I realize that I couldn't think at all; I am not able to think rationally. How should I behave these days? Sometimes it can be weeks like that. Pure stress. Sodom and Gomorrah—this is what happens on Wall Street these days. The folks who could keep themselves, like you and Warren, away from it are very intelligent value investors. There are not so many of them unemotional people like that".

## Do Not Become Driven by Ego and Stress. It Causes Dysfunction

Charlie: "Everyone recognizes that sudden stress, for instance from a threat, will cause a rush of adrenaline in the human body, prompting faster and more extreme reaction. And everyone who has taken Psych 101 knows that stress makes social-proof tendency more powerful. In a phenomenon less well recognized but widely known, light stress can slightly improve performance—say, in examination—whereas heavy stress causes dysfunction. But few people know more about heavy stress than it can cause depression. For instance, most people know that an 'acute stress depression' makes thinking dysfunctional because it causes extreme pessimism, often extended in length and usually accompanied by activity-stopping fatigue. Fortunately, as most people know, such a depression is one of mankind's more reversible ailments. Even before modern drugs were available, many people afflicted by depression, such as Winston Churchill and Samuel Johnson, gained great achievement in life. Most people know very little about man's depressive mental breakdowns influenced by heavy stress. But there is at least one exception, involving the work of Pavlov when he was in his seventies and eighties. Pavlov had won the Nobel Prize early in life by using dogs to work out the physiology of digestion. Then he became world-famous by working out more—association responses in dogs, initially salivating dogs—so much so that changes in behavior triggered by more association, like those caused by much modern advertisement, are today often said to come from 'Pavlovian conditioning.' What happened to cause Pavlov lost work was especially interesting. During the great Leningrad flood of the 1920s, Pavlov had many dogs in cages. Their habits had been transformed, by a combination of his 'Pavlovian conditioning' plus standard reward responses, into distinct and different patterns. As the water of the flood came up and receded, many dogs reached a point where they had almost no air space between their noses and the tops of their cages. This subjected them to maximum stress. Immediately thereafter, Pavlov noticed that many of the dogs were no longer behaving as they had. The dog that formerly had liked his trainer now disliked him, for example. This result reminds me one of modern cognition reversals in which a person's love of his parents suddenly becomes hate, as now love has been shifted suddenly to a cult.

"The unanticipated, extreme changes in Pavlov's dogs would have driven any good experimental scientist into a near frenzy of curiosity. That was indeed Pavlov's reaction. But not many scientists would have done what Pavlov next did[lxxxvi]."

Peter: "Oh that is me. That is all about me," said Peter smiling. "I am not so proud to confirm it in myself, I tell you frankly. I like you so much, especially when you were telling me these practical tendency stories. Even before you make such a serious face, if I am a dog, I am an aggressive one, Charlie. I bite very strongly if somebody would like to steal my food or I lose my money. But why am I telling you all this stuff? Maybe it wasn't what you came here with a single aim to teach us, but that is what it is. You amaze me! You know I hate to lose, especially to people like you over intelligence, over perfection."

## Do Not Become Ensnared by Your Own Ego.
## Control Your Emotions

Mr. Brown: "This is all this is, your jealousy, Peter, feelings of envy. Leave that for now. Ok, the dog is biting. What is so special in it?"

"He, he." Peter was smiling. "If I win I can bite as well but not so strong, but if I lose..."

Charlie: "Well, the quality of man's pleasure from a ten-dollar gain does not exactly match the quantity of his displeasure from a ten-dollar loss. That is, the loss seems to hurt much more than the gain seems to help. Moreover, if a man almost gets something he greatly wants and has it jerked away from him at the last moment, he will react much as if he had long owned the reward and had it jerked away. I include the natural human reactions to both kinds of loss experience—the loss of the pos-sessed—reward and the loss of the almost— possessed reward— under one description, Deprival —Superreaction Tendency[lxxxvii]."

Peter: "You have to be a psychologist or professor at the university, Charlie. But does what you told have any practical meaning? How could you prove it? Any examples? I have friends who are even worse than me if they are losing. It is like the end of the world. If they have something on their way, they could destroy it easily. You know that, right. They could practically become very aggressive. Once it happened: one guy lost a huge amount and after that invited me for drinks. You know he was so disappointed I decided to help, you know, as a human being. But believe me, Charlie, if I hadn't run away, then he'd have simply murdered me."

"Have you told him something bad? Why?" Mr. Brown responded carefully, but with curiosity. "What do you think, Charlie: is there any explanation for such behavior?"

Charlie: "The Mungers once owned a tame and good-natured dog that displayed the canine version of Deprival Superreaction Tendency. There was only one way to get bitten by this dog. And that was to try and take some food away from him after he already had it in his mouth. If you did that, this friendly dog would automatically bite. He couldn't help it. Nothing could be more stupid than for the dog to bite his master, but the dog couldn't help being foolish. He had an automatic Deprival Superreaction Tendency in his nature.

"Humans are much the same as this Munger dog. A man ordinarily reacts with irrational intensity to even a small loss, or threatened loss, of property, love, friendship, dominated territory, opportunity, status, or any other valued thing. As a natural result, bureaucratic infighting over the threatened loss of dominated territory often causes immense damage to an institution as a whole. This factor, among others, accounts for much of the wisdom of Jack Welch's long fight against bureaucratic ills of General Electric. Few business leaders have ever conducted wiser campaigns[xxxviii]."

Peter himself was extremely engaged to know Charlie's opinion, to know what Charlie had to say. He was occupied by his own thoughts. His questions and doubts were like an automatic reaction rather than a real interest.

Peter: "I have to tell you one more story, dear gentlemen, about when I was a real dog. For some reason I was raised in a family where the family values were ignored. I don't want you even to know: when I was sixteen, I ran away from home. So, for a long time I hadn't any contact with them at all. One month before I was due to visit my family after ten years apart, I learned that my father had died. Nobody told me that, even my crazy brother. Nobody from my family had sent me a notice, you know; not even my mother. They did not inform me about the inheritance; they tried to hide all of the money—nothing for me. They wanted to leave me as if I were a dog! After that, I was sick for a long time, and then I stayed at my uncle's house for some years. Don't you think I deserved that money? I could never forgive them, for what they had done to me. I lost a lot of my father's inheritance, maybe one million or two, what hell with this money. I lost respect from myself, but this is my brother who made it with me. I couldn't blame my mother as she was a really old woman. Why she couldn't send me a notice? The loss of the money, which was stealing from my own brother. I could even send him to prison, but I did not do that. And of course, I started my life again—lost, completely lost.

I don't know why I am telling you my stories, gentlemen. Maybe because it was my biggest-ever loss. And I am a weak man…couldn't forget my brother."

Mr. Brown kept his eyes on Peter and steered the conversation back to the topic at hand.

Mr. Brown: "Charlie, apart from Peter's personal stories, I am very interested to know if you ever experienced a loss from deprival super-reaction. I am just so curious."

## If You Get a Big Bet, Make It Really Big

Charlie: "Yes, I myself, the would-be instructor here, many decades ago made a big mistake caused in part by the subconscious operation of deprival super-reaction tendency. A friendly broker called and offered me 300 shares ridiculously underpriced, very thinly traded Belridge Oil at $115 per share, which I purchased using cash I had on hand. The next day he offered me 1,500 more shares at the same price, which I declined to buy partly because I could only have made the purchase had I sold something or borrowed the required $173,000.

That was a very irrational decision. I was a well-to-do man with no debt; there was no risk of loss; and similarly no-risk opportunities were not likely to come along. Within two years, Belridge Oil sold out to Shell at price of about $3,700 per share, which made me about $5.4 million poorer, from an opportunity point of view, than I would have been had I then been psychologically acute. As this tale demonstrates, psychological ignorance can be very expensive[lxxxix]".

"I also told commented on this in my recent interview with Forbes:

"In those days, Belridge was a pink-sheet company. It was very valuable. It had a huge oil field, it wasn't ever leased, they owned everything, they owned the land, they owned the oil field, everything. It had liquidating value way higher than the per share price—maybe three times. It was just an incredible oil field that was going to last a long time, and it had very interesting secondary and tertiary recovery possibilities, and they owned the oil field to do whatever they wanted with it. That is rare, too.

"Why in the hell did I turn down the second block of shares I was offered? Chalk it up to my head up a place where it shouldn't be. So that's why I made that decision. It was crazy. So if any of you made such dumb decisions, you should feel very comfortable. You can survive few. It was a mistake of omission, not commission, but it probably cost me $300 to $400 million. I just tell you the story to make you feel good about whatever investment mischances you have had in your own life. I never found a way of avoiding them all[xc]."

Peter: "I understand it, Charlie. It couldn't be a worse feeling than that. I have experienced that as well. For me it couldn't be any worse. I will try to explain. For example, last winter I was in debt—you know, very unpleasant stuff. It is so silly. I was leveraged in risky stocks. I just hoped my stocks would go up to pay my debts back, but it did not happen. I was suffering mentally; maybe even suffering physical injuries are better than the feeling I had. Maybe you have pain and then in a week or month you forget about it. I had put in my money, so I had no cash at a hand. It was such a terrible feeling. If something happened to me, some bad incident, it would have been even better; you will not get all of this shame and pressure. You know sometimes you see on TV some criminals kill each other and that is it. This seemed less painful compared to this enormous pressure. At that time, I hadn't had any friends who could help, and you know it: if you are really in trouble, everybody runs away from you. I was mad, absolutely mad. I was guilty myself."

The waiter brought some water.

Mr. Brown: "Peter, do you want some water or something else?"

Peter: "No thanks. I was thinking these days; I will never laugh again at all…"

## Betting and Gamble Is Mostly a Male Game

Mr. Brown: "Well I was hearing even worse stories. But what is the problem with Wall Street, Charlie? I have a feeling your rationality is quite different from them. And they are mostly male, so it is a male game?"

Charlie: "By and large, and it's interesting to think about. It's mostly a male game. The nuts who did most of this damage are male. You go into a trading room on Wall Street, and you won't find many women barking into the phones and going to the strip clubs.

"There is a lot of testosterone in our present troubles, and of course, the people that get promoted logically are sort of like the people that win our athletic contests and get to be captain of the teams. Many of you were in investment management; you know how it works. Everybody wants the guy that everybody else trusts, who can't stand to lose, that everybody likes, and tends to get things done—and I just described the captain of the team and so forth. There is a law firm in town, Latham and Watkins, that galloped past everyone else, and that is all they would hire with some exceptions. They knew what they wanted and, boy, did it work for them. Of course, if you are in investment management, it's exactly the wrong personality type. Maybe you want them in the sales department, but you don't want them managing the money. It's the cranky peculiar people like those sitting here who will better serve you in making these decisions. That is another problem with life. [The] guy who invented the Peter Principle is right: You know we all get promoted in hierarchies and, of course, half the time some guy gets one category too high and of course half the time you have someone who is utterly unqualified for this spot he is sitting in and yet he has the power. He's got a big ego and everything else. What do you do about this? This is a serious problem. If you don't think this is a problem with Wall Street look at the personality profiles of the people that headed our main investment banks. They were caricatures. Stan O'Neal or whatever his name was at Merrill—

If [Antony] Trollope invented a character like this, you would say, 'It's too extreme. I can't get by with this one.' It would be regarded as foolish, not effective satire. That just happened again and again and again.

And you are surprised we have this big mess on our hands. Some very powerful forces have been unleashed here. Some very powerful forces of unreason have been allowed to flourish. Of course we get a big mess. We always were going to have cyclical fluctuations in security markets. But to have them magnified so greatly, and to have such exacerbation of the result by this extremely liberal use of credit[xci]."

Mr. Brown: "I think I've got a final conclusion, gentleman, but I still don't understand myself. Money managers are people, well-educated people, otherwise they would not be on Wall Street. They have clients who trust them with their money. It is impossible for these clients to find out about investing opportunities on their own. You know, not everybody is comfortable with it. We can see clearly from the facts that they are earning the money for their clients on a commission basis. Partly these money managers have families; there are children and infants to take care of. They couldn't provide their services for nothing, you know. It is absolutely legal, legal gambling. I see it from perspective of man of the twenty-first century, so I don't see a big problem in speculation. I don't care about these human sufferings, and if it is useful for our civilization or not, if one is stupid enough to play his own money and life. I don't want it to be fully controlled by the government, because the gambler who is stupid will destroy him or herself anyway, or they will learn something from it. I like the idea of gambling. I like to play. There must have been an idea why this feeling is so strong; it is more powerful than anything else. Once you are inside, there is no way back. This idea of easy money: where I think it is not that easy will always be in people's mind, and what the hell could be without it? It is boring to be rational. And I say yes, the value investors, well, some of them like Charlie, they are just luckier than others. They are luckier to be born in the right place at the right time, they are also born gamblers and not engineers like Peter or construction workers, or a farmer, well I'm drunk, but I tell the truth! Where is the power? Who could change the rules? Show me a force who is going to change this gambling, and how? Are there morality and principles in gambling? There are no borders and people's morality. Everything is so relative. The point now is you are my guests. I respect you highly, Charlie, as a human being and as a value investor, but you are a rarity, and all of these idiots, and they are the majority."

Charlie smiled and had nothing to add. Well, he could speak a lot about greed and envy on Wall Street, but today he was thinking it was enough. "When I reach the idea, the sun will probably rise, and some people will find it useful." However, he definitely couldn't argue people to be more intelligent than they have to be. "I shall never lie, looking directly on these issues. But this is my perspective for me and my life. I would certainly be very happy to close this casino of Wall Street or make the rules much stricter; allowing the participant to make some bets every year or something like that. And what would Franklin do about it?" Charlie was always looking for solutions of simplicity, to look at it under the prism of different mental models. If he was contemplating issues, he had a talent for switching everything else out. The room where he was sitting was with eminent dead people who were just sitting there, reminding him of ideas and principles. Charlie just had to come through this checklist on ethics. Yes, first morality and ethics; everything else was next.

Charlie was a little tipsy after only two glasses of wine, but he was in good spirits. He caught Mr. Brown's eye and gave him a friendly smile.

"Just tell me, dear Charlie, have you ever forced yourself on something?" Mr. Brown said all of a sudden, changing the subject completely, to Charlie's surprise.

"I've noticed," said Charlie, "you have taken a great interest in my personality, so it seems I am right."

Mr. Brown: "Yes I am. You can add that I've enough of my own way of thinking about my present situation in life, my work. But I am very interested in your refreshing thoughts, dear Charlie."

At the same time, everybody in the room noticed that Peter was completely drunk. He was sitting quiet, now suddenly awake as if somebody told him some horrible news or shouted at him. His face was pale. Peter was looking at Charlie's face.

Peter: "Are you a devoted Christian? Nobody heard you call yourself a Christian."

Charlie looked at him but did not reply.

Peter: "You are not going to answer? You think I like all of your stories, dear Charlie?"

Charlie: "No, I don't think so. I know you don't like me. I knew it from yesterday you didn't like me."

Peter: "That's because I am jealous of you, of your skills and money. You have always known that, but...but why am I telling you all this? I want some more champagne. Could somebody give me another glass?"

Mr. Brown pushed the glass away from him.

Peter: "You are right. People may say...who the hell cares what they say? You know how often I have a dreamed that I am nobody you know. What an awful dream I have. I wish Charlie would have dreams like me. I have no skills, no money, and I'm homeless, without work, lost. Anyway, if you don't like me, you will not wish me any harm, correct? You are so polite and intelligent. And I am nothing, nothing. This is who I am. Skills I have: zero. Why do I keep asking questions, always asking you questions?"

Mr. Brown jumped from his chair suddenly and unexpectedly trying to stop Peter from speaking.

Mr. Brown: "Peter, you are too drunk to continue this conversation. You are not capable of thinking right now, I believe."

Peter looked around the table with the same aggressive sincerity. "But really, Charlie, that is astonishing. It is an incredible phenomenon, Charlie. I envy other people; I envy you. I mostly hate all of the guests in this room," he repeated. "You may have noticed, Charlie; I know you collect all of these notes and information on psychological misjudgments...I am not forcing anyone to listen!" He sat down on a sofa with his hands on his face. It was silent.

Peter continued: "All of these people, with their luxury properties, suits, and everyone shows you suits they wear." He started to shout. "I work like a horse, all day. I am poor and I will die hungry like a dog on the street. Others don't have to work; they just sit and read all the time. They are polite and educated, yet they're rich! These people, they have no heart. If you meet one of them on the street. If you talk to them like, 'Oh I am so poor and hungry; my life is miserable; I couldn't afford to buy the medicine; my child, my first daughter, was kept in a hospital after she was born because we couldn't have her.'" He caught his breath for a moment. "And what do you think they will answer you? Something like 'oh I never have any pity for that idiot.' Why am I not Buffett myself? Whose fault is it? I was born to be an opposite of Charlie Munger? Yes, I was turned out on the streets when I was young, hardly clothed and a hungry young boy, but healthy—then I would have shown them."

Charlie: "What do you want to show them?"

Mr. Brown: "Well, that is enough from you for today, Peter. It is just enough for today. You have to go home, you know. I am apologizing to all of my guests for this incident." He took Peter's elbow and supported him to the entrance hall. After Mr. Brown returned to the room, he decided to continue the conversation despite what had just happened minutes before."

Mr. Brown: "Peter's story and his statements get on my nerves. Apparently, the person would like to imitate Jesus Christ. He is a nice young person but sometimes goes too far in his own conclusions. Peter could copy so many ideas; he is full of skills, but stubborn, if you under-stand what I mean. I hope with time he will be much better, well he has to be…I kept trying to encourage him to work more and longer on his skills and discipline, but it is his own choice and fault, this self-pity attitude. He prefers every time I speak to fight back at me, all the time.

"Once I saw him very hysterical. I told him it was his own fault to behave like that. I had to explain him. He was really angry and not ratio-nal, like an animal he was—so aggressive; no rationality, just blind. He was losing his temper and told me to leave his home. But I do believe he understood what I meant exactly. It is so much easier to make someone guilty than to learn the truth yourself. But I was very sure that he would apologize for his angry and shameful behavior. Then I decided to leave him alone. Peter is definitely a smart person. But Charlie, why do so many smart people get it wrong?"

Charlie: "Well, that is a marvelous question, and it is such a marvelous question that I have devoted a big chunk of my life to studying that exact question. It was obvious to me for some reason, at an early age, that a great many very brilliant and disciplined people made perfectly screwy decisions that were disastrous—and that happens, frankly, wherever I look. I found it extremely curious, and somehow early in life I got the idea that I would never be able to play chess blindfolded against six Grandmasters and win. God just did not give Charlie Munger any such skill. But I said, 'Oh gosh, I cannot be as asinine as all these other people if I just kind of work at it steadily for a long time,' and that is what I did.

I think part of the popularity of Berkshire Hathaway is that we look like people who have found a trick. It's not brilliance. It's just avoiding stupidity. You say it is the same thing just stated differently—well, maybe it is the same thing just started differently. But you understand it better if you go at it the way we do, which is to identify the main stupidities that do bright people in and then organize your patterns for thinking and developments, so you don't stumble into those stupidities[xcii]."

## Recognize Reality Even When You Do Not Like It. Especially When You Do Not Like It

Charlie: "Recognize reality even when you don't like it—especially when you don't like it"[xciii].

Mr. Brown: "Yes, this is exactly the point, Charlie, but what I notice is that there are some people who take an enormous pleasure in being offended, you know. I will try to explain to you. Well, Peter believes we are deeply guilty in his own faults. From time to time, I meet such people. They are intelligent enough to understand their own faults, but they are somewhat delighted by the chance to tell somebody their crazy bitter stories, to find somebody guilty of all his failures. They are so mysterious; they just need a 'victim' to speak with others. The same is the case on Wall Street. The guy who lost everything, he has no idea about it because of greed. They go into debt, so you know the rest is history, right?"

### Learn Form Viktor E. Frankl: Man's Searching for a Meaning

Charlie: "Yes, this is the correct idea. I will not stop repeating one of my favorite books, one of which is Viktor E. Frankl's *Man's Search for Meaning*[xciv]. In that book, Frankl wrote: 'When we are no longer able to change a situation, we are challenged to change ourselves... Everything can be taken from a man but one thing: the last of the human freedoms— to choose ones attitude in any given set of circumstances, to choose one's own way[xcv].'" So, Peter definitely sees himself as a victim.

"Whenever you think that something or some person is ruining your life, it's you. A victimization mentally is so debilitating. It is actually you who are ruining your life... feeling like a victim is a perfectly disastrous way to go through life. If you just take the attitude that however bad it is in any way, it's always your fault and you just fix it as best as you can—the so called 'iron prescription'—I think that really works."

Mr. Brown: "Yes, I understand it; I could see this attitude could work, Charlie. But when you see a lot of people coming to New York City from all around the country to work here, full of hopes, but some of them are angry and envious, full of self-pity."

Charlie: "Generally speaking, envy, resentment, revenge, and self-pity are disastrous modes of thoughts. Self-pity gets pretty close to paranoia, and paranoia is one of the very hardest things to reverse. You do not want to drift into self-pity[xcvi]."

Shortly after Charlie was speaking, moments of his life rose in his memory. It was 1953 when Charlie was divorced from his wife. He was a young man, twenty-nine years old. When he married for the first time, he was twenty-one. After a very painful divorce, he suffered enormously; his wife kept the family in their house in South Pasadena. During this time, Charlie was driving a big old car, a yellow Pontiac. He moved to small home at the University Club. One day was worse than the others were, as he found out his son, Teddy, was ill with leukemia. These times were hard times as Charlie had to pay for medical treatments of his son, and the death rate was near 100 percent since doctors at that time had no effective treatment. Charlie was struggling a lot with his life. One of his nearest friends, Rick Guerin, said later that Charlie would go into the hospital, hold his young son, and then walk the streets of Pasadena crying. In 1955 Teddy Munger died. Charlie was thirty-one years old, divorced, broke and burying his nine-year-old son. He noticed all of this suffering made him a better person. Unforgettable life stories had made him more rational. One of those moments Charlie was thinking was the hardest. It was the process of losing a son step by step and being unable to help him[xcvii].

## Charlie: It Is Time for Me to Learn Braille.
## Move On and Make a Change

Another story Charlie was thinking about was that recently he was developing a condition in his remaining eye that was causing it to fill up with blood. He would eventually go blind in this remaining eye and lose his eyesight completely. Blindness. When you are an obsessive reader like Charlie, losing your ability to see would seem like a prison sentence. However, Charlie was undeterred. He told someone close to him, "It's time for me to learn braille." He has been taking braille lessons since. Most recently, the worrisome eye condition had receded, but the story is a good example of Charlie's philosophy on life. No self-pity. No emotional wallowing. Staying rational. It is hard enough to learn new things, but…[xcviii]

Charlie: "I think I developed courage when I learned I could deal with hardship. You need to get your feet wet and get some failures under your feet[xcix]."

Mr. Brown: "Well, I don't know why, but I want to tell you my story about an experience I had several years ago. You know I have two sons. At that time one of them was five and another seven years old. We had this beautiful house in my parents' village; we used to live there during the summer. Beautiful lake, fresh air—it could not be better for kids. At that point, I wanted them to know what a normal life was, village life. Simple family homes, folk do not have much money to spend—a little different compared to city life, big-city life. And people of course are more kind and sincere—honest, hardworking families. My boy one morning found a dog dying near our house. It was a beautiful black dog, maybe three or four months old. Somebody had poisoned her or something, as there were no visible injuries to the body. Johnny, my oldest boy, took care of her and fed her milk. We took her to see a doctor. Then we learned that in the neighboring house was a young boy who was ill all the time. He was mostly in his bed. It turned out this dog was his only friend, and he was crazy not to lose it. It was a big family, I believe four or five kids. We visited their house one day when Johnny learned about where his dog had come from. When he returned home, he was so sad he did not want to return the dog, but he understood that he had to help that little ill boy, and he returned the dog right away. After that, we decided to visit this family with some toys and amuse this little boy a little. But every time we came the boy was pale and had no energy to get up. Johnny wanted to help the boy and we even called our doctor to come from New York City to visit him. But the doctor could only tell us that the boy had several months to live, no more. The family was so sad. His dad was crying but never showed the little boy his emotions. He just repeated to him: 'Dear John, you will be better soon, I know. I know it.' But he was knew it was just not true. The boy was dying. When Johnny brought his dog to John, the boy was so glad; he even stood up, hugged it, and smiled. After a week, we visited him again, and he did not want to speak, just lay in bed. Life is really tough from time to time."

## Life Is Tough. If You Can Handle It You Have Won

Charlie: "Assume life will be really tough, and then ask if you can handle it. If the answer is yes, you've won. You need to keep raw, irrational emotion under control. You need patience and an ability to take losses and adversity without going crazy[c]."

Charlie was walking in Mr. Brown's big beautiful park, thinking of the similarity of human suffering. Those thoughts were prevented by the pounding of his heart. Inside his head there were too many thoughts; he couldn't stop it.

But it was soon not possible to think. He regretted some moments in his life, while other moments made him happy. He wished sometimes to be indifferent to a person or a situation. Sometimes he wanted to be unable to give comment or to answer the questions. From time to time, he was tormented by his emotions, but nobody had to know about it. He understood this even in childhood, but he had trained himself to stay rational as an adult. When he was feeling the reality and the world around was crazy, he could not stop it, but he could manage his emotions. He was thinking about Omaha and one of the sunny days, when he was a child waking up, with bright sun coming through the window. Every morning there was a rainbow, and he knew it. Everything was calm and quiet. He knew nothing and comprehended nothing—no people, no sounds, just a feeling of happiness surrounded by his family and friends. Sometimes he regretted some words and statements, but he had not been able to say that differently. He had to be honest, direct, and rational.

After he returned from his walk, he was sitting around the table with guests; he noticed Mr. Brown's wife came to sit near him in order to continue the dialogue.

Mrs. Brown's wife: "Charlie, we have already heard a lot of your stories yesterday. I regard you as an extremely honest and truthful man. I am not able to compare you with somebody else. You are truthful and direct. People criticize you sometimes for your straightforwardness, but not me. I will never criticize you or that sort of thing. I do believe and understand this is the correct way of dealing with adversities of any kind. It is very interesting to discuss with you all these topics, without any exception. I would like to know your position and the biggest mistakes you've made and losses you've had, both in private and in business. I have to know them all. Could you please tell us your stories? I have heard that once somebody said to begin with a prayer. If you begin with a prayer, you can think more clearly and will make fewer mistakes.

"I believe the faults topic is not the easiest to discuss, but sometimes you are so passionately objective in everything you are doing, Charlie. I believe you could be speaking with some affection on everything. I have made one of the biggest mistakes recently; I put a lot of my money into gold. I have a friend, a banker; he told me that it was a correct decision. You know I am not a professional investor, but when I visit my friend, the banker, I am too tired of that kind of stuff to make a decision myself; it is too complex. I always believe I do not understand anything of that value investing. I just want to trust somebody to do the job for me. I just remember I visited him. I do remember everything he talked about, in fact what both of us talked about. I had a lot of cash, and I just didn't know where to put it all. I was so worried that somebody should steal it. I decided to bury it, into gold first, then into the ground. I have heard that Buffett once said, 'Gold gets dug out of the ground in Africa, or someplace. Then we melt it down and dig another hole, bury it again and pay people to stand around guarding it. It has no utility. Anyone watching from Mars would be scratching their head[ci].' But I have no ideas myself of how to manage it. In the end, he advised me that instead of wastefully invested into any risky stocks; I should take it to charity. I made it partly. When I did it, I had a very nice feeling: you know, help children who are in need. And when I remember and realize the suffering on the faces of these small babies, their eyes full of worship for me, how I could not believe them, looking at such children? If one sees into the eyes of these children, one sees clearly hopes and almost believes in miracles, that one day some person will come and save them.

"So, this was my story, I never regret giving the money to charity, if it is managed well and honestly. But I still believe it was very stupid to put the rest of my money into gold. I believe it was a mistake."

### Gold Is Stupid. Invest into Productive Businesses

Charlie kept silent for a moment, then answered, "I think gold is a great thing to sew into your garments if you're a Jewish family in Vienna in 1939, but I think civilized people don't buy gold. They invest into productive businesses[cii]."

Mr. Brown: "I think last year I read a very clear definition of failure from Warren Buffett. He was asked, 'Mr. Buffet, how did you first get started and how did you deal with a failure, if you had one?'

"Buffett answered, 'How did I first get started? It depends. I bought my first stock when I was eleven, but I'd been thinking about them for a long time before that. My dad was in the investment business, and I used to go down to his office in the old Omaha National Bank building when I was seven or eight years old. I found out I was near-sighted because I couldn't read the quotations up on the board; otherwise I might have gone through life without glasses. I just got very interested in it. I started reading books on it when I was eight or nine and then I finally saved enough money to buy three shares of Cities Service Preferred for $114 in 1942, and then I just kept doing it.

"'Failure depends on how you define it. A lot of things go wrong in life, but that doesn't necessarily mean that they're failures. I really don't look back. I try to learn from what I see around me, but I don't try to learn by going back over this decision or that decision or what did I do wrong or that sort. I don't think about that at all. You can make a lot of mistakes. The nice thing about it is you are going to make a lot of mistakes and still do very well. That's the encouraging thing. I write about my mistakes in the report. In fact, I have a section sometimes called "mistake du jour" and unfortunately its plural most years, too. It's not the end of the world. You don't want to make any mistakes that are fatal. You do not want to own securities on borrowed money because that can wipe you out. But there is nothing wrong with making mistakes. You should try to pick things that you understand. That is the key to what I do. Occasionally I may make a mistake when I think I understand something I don't. Another mistake that you don't see is when I pass up something that I'm capable of understanding. Those are mistakes of omission, and sometimes they have been huge. I could point to mistakes like that which have cost us over a billion dollars. I know enough to do something but for a reason or another, I didn't. Fortunately, people don't see those[ciii].'"

### Learning from Your Mistakes and Doing Your Homework Will Deepen Your Experience

Charlie: "You can learn to make mistakes, but you can learn to make fewer of them than other people and fix your mistakes faster when you do make them. But there is no way that you can live an adequate life without making many mistakes. The trick is to get so you can handle mistakes.

Part of what you must learn is how to handle mistakes and new facts that change the odds. Failure to handle psychological denial is a common way for people to go broke: You've made an enormous commitment to something. You've poured effort and money in. And the more you put in, the more the whole consistency principle makes you think, 'Now it has to work.' If I put in a little more, then it will work.' I basically advise you to use two-track analysis. First, what are the factors that really govern the interests involved, rationally considered? And second, what are the sub-conscious influences where the brain, at a subconscious level, is auto-matically doing these things—which by and large are useful, but which often malfunction. One approach is rationality. The other is to evaluate the psychological factors that cause subconscious conclusions[civ]."

It was the last evening for Charlie to be in New York City. Tomorrow he was due to take the train back to Omaha, and he never saw these people again.

# Chapter Two

## Charlie and Benjamin Franklin

To understand how Charlie thinks, one must understand his rules and personality. He is always inner-directed and mostly indifferent to the opinion of others. From an early age, Charlie was hated in the university for his direct opinion, but he does not need any approval from others. If a problem or mistake has great complexity, he tries to consider it with a multidisciplinary approach, trying first to simplify the problem. He does not possess any impulsiveness to give the answer; his extraordinary approach involves thinking and concentrating on a problem. His mind could not be compared to somebody else's.

In business, Charlie would like to ensure from the beginning of making any decision that he knows the rules. Like in bridge, he is not playing to be beaten. He is self-disciplined in every detail and calm to beat the odds. When he has a plan for action, he brings easy and quick decisions. The problem or any issue could look complicated, but not for Charlie, who already thought it through and just took it directly right to the point. He devotes a tremendous amount of his time to books, to having the right-thinking tool to apply to any problem or complex situation. One may say that Charlie was trained from the beginning to work, to be disciplined, and to save money. As Benjamin Franklin once said, "A penny saved is a penny earned[cv]." Buffett himself agrees that Berkshire Hathaway was shaped tremendously by the way Charlie approaches practice and discipline; of course, it has a big impact on Warren Buffett as well. At an early age, Charlie took the path of an adult. He has an exaggerated sense of responsibility in everything he does; he took that habit throughout his life. He and Buffett both learned to be survivors of very difficult times when everybody around was stressed and frustrated. Self-devotion to reading is a rarity in the modern business world. Charlie was a college dropout who served as a meteorologist in the US Army Air Corps before graduating from Harvard University. He forced himself to be a learning machine.

## Be Reliable. Do Not Get Distracted by Your Passion

Charlie: "What do you want to avoid? Such an easy answer: sloth and unreliability. If you are unreliable, it doesn't matter what your virtues are; you're going to crater immediately. Doing what you have faithfully engaged to do should be an automatic part of your conduct. You want to avoid sloth and unreliability[cvi]." Charlie idolized his main hero, Benjamin Franklin. From the books, including biographies on Charlie, we could not confirm any evidence that Charlie ever was influenced by gossip or people's opinion. He maintains mostly indifferent to crowd opinion. He trained himself to be like that.

We could not tell when Charlie first felt the interest for reading, turning this interest into a systematic approach to worldly wisdom, but it was clearly from an early age. This quality of his to acquire knowledge with discipline was so consequential for his broad education and development that we must pause briefly to consider it.

Charlie: "I met the towering intellectuals in books, not in the classroom, which is natural. I can't remember when I first read Ben Franklin. I had Thomas Jefferson over my bed at seven or eight. My family was into all that stuff, getting ahead through discipline, knowledge, and self-control." This obsession with learning through his life combined with discipline might seem too strict or even very unusual in today's society, but this discipline kept Charlie busy all the time. Charlie always has books around him when he travels, reading any time he has a minute to spare. He tries to learn everything he can from books[cvii]".

## Learning. Confidence. Decisiveness

Charlie: "Obviously the more hard lessons you can learn vicariously, instead of from your own terrible experiences, the better off you will be. I don't know anyone who did it with great rapidity. Warren Buffett has become one hell of a better investor since the day I met him, and so have I. If we had been frozen at any given stage, with the knowledge we had, the record would have been much worse than it is. So, the game is to keep learning[cviii]." Charlie never aspired to huge popularity at school. Resentment, self-pity—these emotions were not a part of Charlie's character and individuality. Through some stories we may see that he suffers, or he is sensitive to some issues, but usually the emotions are "closed" and under his control. In business, he prefers to have a cold mask of objectivity.

Charlie loves and admires Benjamin Franklin, who has a lot to teach us about ethics, greed, morals, and money. Charlie adopted the multidisciplinary approach in learning from his hero. One could train his brain as a sportsman preparing for the Olympic Games. Charlie is confident that to be smart one has to have a collection of mental models in mind. Just one model, or only a few, is not enough to be an independent thinker.

Charlie: "To the man with only a hammer, every problem looks like a nail[cix]." He thinks that to be prepared to operate in this world, one must have a multidisciplinary education. Charlie requires people to be able to think using multiple mental models.

Benjamin Franklin, according to a published autobiography, said that too much focus on quality of life (materialism) could be result in a lower dysfunctional emotion, which can cause you to pay too much for everything. So, one has to have control over it. One may see a parallel between Franklin and Munger, as exemplified in *Education of Youth in Pennsylvania*[cx].

Franklin: "As to their Studies, it would be well if they could be taught everything that is useful, and everything that is ornament. But art is long, and their time is short. It is therefore proposed that they learn those things that are likely to be most useful and most ornamental. Regard being had to the several professions for which they are intended[cxi]."

Charlie about Franklin: "There is the sheer amount of Franklin's wisdom...and talent. Franklin played four instruments. He was the nation's leading scientist and inventor, plus a leading author, statesman, and philanthropist. There has never been anyone like him...Franklin was quite old when he was ambassador to France. This was after he was world famous and rich, and he was making his way in the world. But he was a very good ambassador, and whatever was wrong with him from John Adams's point of view helped him with the French. I think Franklin was a marvelous steward. I'm willing to take the fellow as he averaged out. And certainly, I'm in favor of old people having a little enjoyment[cxii]." Charlie Munger took such internal monitoring of self-discipline to a new, advanced level. As one may notice through continuously learning and studying people patiently, in such subjects as history and psychology, Charlie is hoping to avoid spontaneity and unpredictability in his life.

## Benjamin Franklin. Reading Was the Only Amusement
## I Allowed Myself

Once Franklin said: "This library afforded me the means of improvement by constant study, for which I set apart an hour or two each day, and thus repaired in some degree the loss of the learned education my father once intended for me. Reading was the only amusement I allowed myself. I spend no time in taverns, going or frolics of any kind, and my industry in my business continued as indefatigable as it was necessary[cxiii]."

Through his straightforwardness, objectivity, and rationality, Charlie tried hard to insulate himself from all unnecessary temptations and emotions. Charlie made a huge effort in collecting and contributing to the business world, where he put all psychological tendencies, typical error-causing mistakes, biases, and faults into "The Psychology of Human Misjudgment." He fully believed that a person should try to avoid all of the bias from tendency. One must also try to avoid fooling himself. He repeatedly announces his favorite quote from Richard Feynman: "The first principle is that you must not fool yourself and you are the easiest person to fool." Charlie is an expert generalist who collects expertise through subjects and discipline; he is both intellectually humble and open to new ideas, as was Benjamin Franklin.

Charlie: "The game is to keep learning, and I don't think people are going to keep learning who don't like the learning." And, "You have to realize the truth of biologist Julian Huxley's idea that 'Life is just one damn relatedness after another. So, you must have the models, and you must see the relatedness and the effects from the relatedness[cxiv].'"

Charlie learned to combine his inside rules to avoid psychological influence and show discipline not only in business. He learned not to show his emotions, not to follow the crowd opinion, and to camouflage his approach, which is from time to time too direct and straightforward, behind a studied calm. These abilities are clearly demonstrated at all Berkshire annual meetings. Calm, independent thinker Charlie.

Even Warren Buffett admits that Charlie has a phenomenal memory, he has an ability to switch everything else out to concentrate on a matter or a problem. The main characteristics of Charlie's portrait is his prudish honesty during his career and life.

## Track Records Are Your Successes. Start It Early

Charlie: "I think track records are very important. If you start early, trying to have a perfect one, in some simple thing like honesty, you're well on your way to success in this world[cxv]."

Charlie Munger handles people with different attitudes. He does not suffer fools at all, and he has no time to make people feel comfortable and please them as Warren Buffett does. He goes right to the point with a smart rationality. He always avoids the events where he has to please people; because of his courage and straightforwardness, he has a lot of haters and critics from Wall Street.

Charlie is independent, brutally honest, and has a sharp wit. If Buffett would like to talk about an issue or a problem through, with a long and detailed explanation to the public and shareholders as to why they acted in a certain way, Charlie would rather cut it to a short version. His rationality and honesty explain his popularity. Individuals who speak the truth are very interesting, funny, and insightful.

Charlie: "If people tell you what you really don't want to hear, what's unpleasant—there is an almost automatic reaction of antipathy. You have to train yourself out of it[cxvi]."

However, he is very persistent with statements that please or displease people according to taste. Charlie Munger is confident that you will lose on everything through your life without a system to make wise decisions.

Charlie: "You don't have to have perfect wisdom to get very rich— just a bit better than the average over a long period of time[cxvii]."

In talking about Wall Street and speculation, frauds, and scandals, Charlie must seem self-possessed and orientated, but he always hears very carefully, what others have to say. However, mostly resistant to the crowd's opinion, and the thoughts of others, he is independent enough to have his own point of view.

Charlie: "Crowd folly, the tendency of humans, under the same circumstances, to resemble lemmings, explains much foolish thinking of brilliant men and much foolish behavior—like investment management practices of many foundations represented here today. It is sad that today each institutional investor apparently fears most of all that its investment practices will be different from the practices of the rest of the crowd[cxviii]."

## Get a Seamless Web of Deserved Trust from People You Are Dealing With

Charlie Munger had an unfailing knack for knowing whom he could trust, and he wanted to deal only with people who got his trust. The most important characteristics of an individual in his opinion are honesty and integrity. So, his wish, in short, was to surround himself with trustworthy, smart people, even or especially if they had different points of view. He said a "seamless web of deserved trust is the most important quality of a person you could ever get[cxix]."

Charlie: "The last idea that I want to give to you, as you go out into a profession that frequently puts a lot of procedure and some mumbo jumbo into what it does, is that complex bureaucratic procedure do not represent the highest form civilization can reach. The highest form that civilization can reach is a seamless web of deserved trust. Not much fancy procedure, just totally reliable people correctly trusting one another. That's the way an operating room works at Mayo Clinic. If lawyers were to introduce a lot of lawyer like process, more patients would die. So never forget, when you are a lawyer, that while you may to sell procedure, you don't have to buy. In your own life, what you want is a seamless web of deserved trust. And if your proposed marriage contract has forty-seven pages, I suggest is you not enter[cxx]."

## Warren Buffett and Charlie Munger

As we know from other sources, after meeting Warren Buffett in 1959, Charlie was impressed by him. As it turned out later, Buffett already had his trust from the beginning of their friendship. The partnership between Warren Buffett and Charlie Munger has had a huge importance for the further development of Berkshire Hathaway. Munger had a significant influence over Buffett's point of view, including capital allocation. In a long career, we could not recognize a concurrence or a dominance over each other. One may say what he wants, but objectively these two men have influenced each other in the best way possible. As the strongest part of Charlie's character was a silent craft and a habit of avoiding any predictions, quiet and objective, mostly passionate, he got the nickname "a silent partner." As we see from Berkshire's annual meeting in 2016, which was video recorded for the first time in history, in answering questions Charlie, with impermeable poise, showed no sign of being upset or disappointed—a reflection of his lifelong habit to keep emotions under control. Buffett gave very detailed answers as usual while Charlie gave short, sharp answers of two or three sentences. As mentioned earlier, Charlie and Warren want to be surrounded by only trustworthy people who can inspire confidence. Therefore, management of Berkshire businesses are not controlled by quarterly earnings releases from Omaha.

Charlie: "We have an extreme centralization at headquarters where a single person makes all the capital allocation decisions, and we have decentralization among our operations without a big bureaucracy. That's the Berkshire Hathaway model[cxxi]."

Charlie: "Good character is very efficient. If you can trust people, your system can be way simpler. There is enormous efficiency in good character and disefficiency in bad character[cxxii]." Charlie understands clearly that when trust exists, you can maximize efficiency and productivity. As one may see, you can avoid a lot of craziness and inefficiency only based on this rule, to only deal with persons who are trustworthy.

## Buffett: Charlie and My Task Is to Attract and Keep
## Outstanding Managers

Charlie: "We want people where every aspect about their personality makes you want to be around them. Trust first, ability second[cxxiii]." He is a strong believer in "you couldn't make a good deal with a bad person[cxxiv]." He draws a characteristic conclusion: "A lot of people think if you just had more process and more compliance-checks and double-checks and so forth—you could create a better result in the world. Well, Berkshire has had practically no process. We had hardly any internal auditing until they forced it on us. We just try to operate in a seamless web of deserved trust and be careful whom we trust[cxxv]." And he says, "I think your best compliance cultures are the ones which have this attitude of trust and some of the ones with the biggest compliance departments, like Wall Street, have the most scandals[cxxvi]." As Buffett put it: "Charles T. Munger, Berkshire Hathaway's vice-chairman, and I really have only two jobs…One is to attract and keep outstanding managers to run our various operations. The other is capital allocation."

Charlie at Daily Journal Corporation Meeting in 2014: "When you get a seamless web of deserved trust, you get enormous efficiencies…Every once in a while, it doesn't work, not because someone's evil but because somebody drifts to inappropriate behavior and then rationalizes it.

"There is money in being trusted. It's such a simple idea, and yet everybody rushes into every scummy activity that seems to work."

They are avoiding the men of questionable reputation. Buffett and Munger are already rich and can therefore afford to not to deal with people with a bad attitude, or to put it simply, bad people. This extraordinary partnership between Charlie Munger and Warren Buffett is significant for the foundation and development of Berkshire; we will discover this in detail later. However, from their point of view any person who has no trust is a weak person without morality and honesty and is thus destined to be a poor businessperson. Wall Street people have opposite values such as greed, envy, and speculation. As Buffett said at BRK 2014: "Sandy Gottesman, a guy in the construction business in Omaha shared with me this story on risk control. Sandy had fired one of his staff who said, 'How can you fire me—I'm one of your best producers!' Sandy replied, 'But I am a rich old man, and you make me nervous.'"

## Best Move Is to Be Calm and Reliable

I will focus on this issue as I think it has a significant importance to our story. Charlie: "First, be unreliable. Do not faithfully do what you have engaged to do. If you will only master this one habit, you will more than counterbalance the combined effect of all your virtues, howsoever great. If you like being distrusted and excluded from the best human contribution and company, this prescription is for you. Master this one habit, and you will always play the role of the hare in the fable except that instead of being outrun by one fine turtle you will be outrun by hordes and of mediocre turtles and even by some mediocre turtles on crutches.

"I must warn you that if you don't follow my first prescription, it may be hard to end up miserable even if you start disadvantaged. I had a roommate in college who was and is severely dyslexic. But he is perhaps the most reliable man I have ever known. He has had a wonderful life so far, outstanding wife and children, chief executive of a multibillion dollar corporation. If you want to avoid a conventional, main-cultural, establishment result of this kind, you simply don't count on your other handicaps to hold you back if you persist in being reliable"[cxxvii].

## Good Behavior Is Productive and Your Only Asset

Charlie: "How you behave in one place will help in surprising ways later." Charlie thinks that the best way to get something is to deserve it. One has to discharge duties faithfully and well.

Charlie: "Well, luckily I had the idea at a very early age that the safest way to try to get what you want is to try to deserve what you want. It's such a simple idea. It's a golden rule. You want to deliver to the world what you would buy if you were on the other end. There is no ethos in my opinion that is better for any lawyer or any other person to have. By and large, the people who've had this ethos win in life, and they don't win just money and honors. They win the respect, the deserved trust of people they deal with. And there is a huge pleasure in life to be obtained from getting deserved trust[cxxviii]."

Potentially escaping from gambling, buying and selling stocks, speculating, and dealing with questionable people is one of the extreme characteristics of Charlie. From the beginning of his career, Charlie never gambled on stock, so we have no records of it.

Charlie: "I knew a guy who had five million and owned his house free and clear. But he wanted to make a bit more money to support his spending, so at the peak of the internet bubble, he was selling puts on the internet stocks. He lost all of his money and his house and now works in a restaurant. It's not a smart thing for the country to legalize gambling [in the stock market] and make it very accessible[cxxix]".

"Gambling does not become wonderful just because it pertains to commerce. It's a casino[cxxx]."

Charlie: "To me, it's obvious that winners have to bet very selectively. It's been obvious to me since very early in life. I don't know why it's not obvious to very many other people[cxxxi]."

Even as a young man, Charlie was extremely well behaved in times of crisis. One could say he has a natural talent to be rational, objective, and passionate about wisdom. The crazier people became, the calmer he was. In his partnership with Buffett, Charlie hasn't ever felt blocked of his opinion by Buffett. Most of the time they agree on every issue and respect each other. With time, the partners already know what the other will think on any issue or problem. So, knowledge accumulation and skill acquisition happen based on personal experiences, but the best way is through the experiences of other people. The rule is for both Buffett and Charlie to read about catastrophes, mistakes other people have made before. To avoid causing pain to yourself, you have to learn it from the mistakes of others.

Charlie: "You don't have to pee on an electric fence to learn not to do it." Both Munger and Buffett consistently stress the importance of learning continually and that continuously applying his mental models approach is essential. Most people, though, don't care about engineering a coherent set of mental models to prepare them to solve everyday issues and problems. What people want, mostly, is to acquire a lot of money.

From Whitney Tilson's note from the 2007 Wesco Annual Meeting:

Charlie: "I want to do something I haven't done before. I feel obligated because so many of you come from such great distances, so I'll talk about a question I've chosen, one that ought to interest you. Why were Warren Buffett and his creation, Berkshire Hathaway, so unusually successful? If that success in investment isn't the best in the history of the investment world, it's certainly the top five. It's a lollapalooza. Why did one man, starting with nothing, no credit rating, end up with this ridiculous collection of assets, $120 billion in cash and marketable securities, all from $10 million when Warren took over, with about the same number of shares outstanding. It's a very extreme result.

"You get some hints if you read *Poor Charlie's Almanack*, which was created by my friend Peter Kaufman, almost against my will—I let him crawl around my office when I wasn't there. He said it would make a lot of money so he put up $750,000 and promised that all profits above this would go to the Huntington Library [one of Munger's favorite charities]. Lo and behold, that's happened. He got his money back, and the donees receiving a large profit. Some people are very peculiar, and we tend to collect them[cxxxii]."

## Warren Is One of the Best Learning Machines on the Earth

Charlie: "A confluence of factors in the same direction caused Warren's success. It's very unlikely that a lollapalooza effect can come from anything else. So, let's look at the factors that contributed to this result. The first factor is the mental aptitude. Warren is seriously smart. On the other hand, he can't beat all comers in chess blindfolded. He is out-achieved his mental aptitude.

"Then there's the good effect caused by his doing this since he was ten years old. It is very hard to succeed until you take the first step in what you are strongly interested in. There is no substitute for strong interest, and he got a very early start. This is really crucial: Warren is one of the best learning machines on Earth. The turtles who outrun the hares are learning machines. If you stop learning in this world, the world rushes right by you. Warren was lucky that he could still learn effectively and build his skills, even after he reached retirement age. Warren's investing skills have markedly increased since he turned sixty-five. Having watched the whole process with Warren, I can report that if he had stopped with what he knew at earlier points, the record would be a pale shadow of what it is.

"The world has been heavily concentrated in one mind. Sure, others have had input, but Berkshire enormously reflects the contributions of one great single mind. It's hard to think of great success by committees in the investment world—or in physics. Many people miss this. Look at John Wooden, the greatest basketball coach ever: his record improved later in life when he got a great idea: be less egalitarian. Of twelve players on his team, the bottom five didn't play—they were just sparring partners. Instead, he concentrated experience in his top players. That happened at Berkshire—there was concentrated experience and playing time. This is not how we normally live in democracy; everyone takes turns. But if you really want a lot of wisdom, it's better to concentrate decisions and process in one person[cxxxiii]."

I am not sure if rationality is the governing principle of the Munger family, but at the same time, I would not be very surprised to learn that he would buy one bicycle for all his children to share one after another.

Charlie, as we read in *Poor Charlie's Almanack*, is a great dad, full of wisdom and extremely gentle with his children, but attached to certain fixed principles and rules, as he is devoted to reading his books and acquiring wisdom.

Charlie's passion is to play bridge and apply its rules in business life, so he can see the possible dangers and at the same time possible opportunities. He has studied bridge to identify the possible combinations that might make him win. He has applied the same rules in business. And it turns out to be a huge success for Warren Buffett to have Charlie as a partner.

If you read Berkshire Hathaway annual reports and interviews with Charlie through the years, you will learn that he made himself one of the finest businesspeople and intellectuals of our time through his morality, honesty, persistence in learning, capacity to think in strategic terms, visionary leadership, and self-control. His had a huge advantage against folks who made everyday decisions and judgements. Depressed atmospheres on markets only strengthened his resolve. This unshakable exalted faith in his own opinion and his own judgement is significant, so in the face of criticism, Charlie is more confident than ever.

As Calvin Coolidge put it: "Nothing in this world can take the place of persistence. Talent will not: nothing is more common than unsuccessful men with talent. Genius will not: unrewarded genius is almost a proverb. Education will not: the world is full of educated derelicts. Persistence and determination alone are omnipotent. The slogan 'Press On' has solved and will always solve the problems of the human race. No person was ever honored for what honor has been the reward for what he gave[cxxxiv]."

## Sit Down on Your Ass Until You Do It

As Charlie puts it: "Another thing you have to do is have a lot of assiduity. I like that word because to me it means: 'Sit down on your ass until you do it. I've had marvelous partners, full of assiduity, all my life. I think I got them partly because I tried to deserve them and partly was shrewd enough to select them, and partly there was some luck. Two partners that I choose for one phase in my life made the following simple agreement when they created a little design/build construction team in the middle of the great depression: 'Two-man partnership,' they said, 'and divide everything equally. And, whenever we're behind in our commitments to other people, we will both work fourteen hours a day, seven days a week, until we're caught up.' Well, needless to say, that firm didn't fail. And my partners were widely admired. Simple, old-fashioned ideas like theirs are almost sure to provide a good outcome[cxxxv]."

However, who cares right now about old-fashioned ideas on Wall Street? With so many losers that are competing with each other in their envy, it's a daily struggle. Only a very few are winners, such as Berkshire Hathaway, and it is therefore no surprise that both Warren Buffett and Charlie Munger have a group of haters and enemies.

As we already know, Charlie is not a big believer in "academic professors" who get to practice only a certain theory, ignoring psychology and multidisciplinary thinking.

Alternatively, there are people whom you call "sentimentalists" or "dreamers[cxxxvi]," who are thinking of the prediction that certain business areas conform to their own competitive models. To buy any stocks, the winner, according to Charlie Munger, bet infrequently. Charlie is famous for waiting and keeping his emotions under control.

Charlie: "It's not given to human beings to have such talent that they can just know everything about everything all the time. But it is given to human beings who work hard at it—who look and sift the world for a mispriced bet that they occasionally find one. And the wise ones bet heavily when the world offers them that opportunity. They bet big when they have the odds. And the rest of the time, they don't. It's just that simple. That is a very simple concept. And to me it's obviously right based on experience not only from the pari-manual system, but everywhere else[cxxxvii]."

Where Charlie Munger is very different from Buffett, who has always been known for the desire to be rich, is that no other businessperson in American history is as well known for his humanity and frugality. When *Forbes* put Charlie Munger on the billionaires' list, Charlie was not happy about it. As a reaction, he donated to his favorite charities to reduce the money on purpose in order not to be included in the *Forbes* list.

## Charlie Is Giving Back. Philanthropy

In 2013, Charlie said: "I'm deliberately taking my net worth down. If it's not below a billion, it soon will be. My thinking is, I'm not immortal. And I won't need it where I'm going. There is nothing as insignificant as an extra $2 billion to an old man.

"I am soon going to be departed from all of my money. Why not give more of it away while I get the fun of giving it?cxxxviii"

Does Charlie differ most from other American businesspeople? The answer is yes. I have not heard of any story in American history where a person felt so firmly about giving back money. He controls the spending to make a real progress. Mostly people just want to outsource the issue to somebody else.

Especially Charlie feels that they have earned their fortune not by being productive, but by being able to pick the right stock. Everybody has a different talent; some are good for art, others for literature. You just have to develop your ability for the good of humankind. Charlie has the ability to make wise capital allocation decisions. He realizes this is a gift he possess, and he has a duty to give back to his own country, use his money rational.

Charlie: "To the extent that all I've done is pick stocks that have gone up and made my family richer, I haven't left much contribution to society. I guess it's a lot like Wall Street. The difference is, I feel ashamed of it." For Charlie Munger, there was a necessity for philosophical and capitalistic wisdom, given his extensive philanthropic work.

In both extensive interviews and comments to WESCO and DJCO, Charlie explained how knowledge and rationality worked out for Berkshire.

At Berkshire's 2008 annual meeting, Warren Buffett said, "You can sell your business to Berkshire, and we'll put it in the Metropolitan museum. It'll have a wing all by itself. It'll be there forever. Or you can sell it to some parts operator, and he'll take the painting and he'll make the boots a little bigger and he'll stick it up the window, and some other guy will come along in the raincoat, and he'll buy it. This is the way Berkshire

has done it: step by step, collecting reputable businesses instead of pur-
suing a disgraceful gambling and mining scheme[cxxxix]."

The cooperation between Charlie Munger and Warren Buffett may
be best described as a couple of a social Darwinists who viewed the
struggle of capitalism in America as a natural process. More often than
other investors, they have seen a great opportunity for Berkshire's growth
and acquisitions.

Charlie, emulating Benjamin Franklin, sees competitive capitalism
not as a materialistic competition only through greed, misguided principles, and dishonesty. Nevertheless, through his prism of rationality,
humanity, morality, and honesty, he has tried to reconcile trust.

## Charlie: The Way to Win Is to Work. Work, Work, and Hope to Have A Few Insights

Charlie: "The way to win is to work, work, work, work, and hope to have a few insights.... And you're probably not going to be smart enough to find thousands in a lifetime. And when you get a few, you really load up. It is just that simple[cxl]." Warren Buffett hired Todd Combs in 2010 and Ted Weschsler in 2011 as part of Berkshire's succession plan, which calls for splitting his job into three parts: an executive chairman; a CEO to handle acquisitions and the core of executives who run Berkshire-owned businesses; and a small group to invest Berkshire money.

Combs, who was born in Australia, one day went to California to see Charlie Munger. Combs remembers thinking, "I'd like to meet Charlie someday[cxli]." He called Munger's office, figuring it was "pretty unlikely" that he would get to see Munger. But Charlie offered to meet him at the California Club for breakfast. "I was terrified," Combs said. He had attended two of Berkshire's annual shareholder meetings in Omaha. He knew that Munger often gave blunt assessments of people and businesses. Combs: "But we really hit it off." He's the warmest gentleman. The two talked for hours and Munger offered to get together again. Combs quickly arranged to return to California. Eventually Munger told him, "I really think Warren would like to meet you."

## Berkshire Hathaway Owner's Manual: Warren Buffett and Charlie Munger

At the same time, Charlie understands the necessity of acting not alone, but in cooperation with other intelligent minds and ideas. Berkshire represents the merger of the two identities of Munger and Buffett to create an empire. Differences of opinion served very well for Berkshire; we do not see any struggles of opinions. Yes, sometimes they may have different opinions, but both sides have a huge mutual respect for each other and are famous for their cordial decisions and strategies. These two together built Berkshire from scratch into a multibillion-dollar company. They did not have money at the beginning, no super technologies not superior information about any particular industry. But they figured out how to fuse together.

The Berkshire Hathaway model is an effective and efficient instrument in Warren Buffett's hands. The partnership of Warren Buffett and Charlie Munger is a combination of the greatest minds of value investors in modern history.

Charlie's mind is, I believe, very special. You can see a continuous thinking process, he is thinking all the time, especially if he focused on a problem or question. He could go away without saying goodbye, as Buffett puts it, as he is completely absorbed in his thinking.

## Concentration Is a Key

Charlie: "Concentrating hard on something that's important, I can't succeed at all without doing it. I did not succeed in life by intelligence. I succeeded because I have a long attention span[cxlii]." Even if Charlie may come across as rude—well, some people consider him rude for what he has to say—but it is because Charlie's mind is occupied constantly and he has his own way of thinking. He can switch off everything around him.

Charlie: "I am a biography nut myself, and I think when you're trying to teach the great concepts that work, it helps to tie them into the lives and personal ties of the people who developed them. I think you learn economics better if you make Adam Smith your friend. That sounds funny, making friends among the eminent dead, but if you go through life making friends with the eminent dead who had the right ideas, I think it will work better in life and work better in education. It's way better than just giving the basic concepts[cxliii]."

This extraordinary ability to see a little further than others makes Charlie superhuman. He is not only a great businessperson and value investor but also has the courage to stick to his own principles when the whole world goes to hell. Patience combined with courage in a moment it is needed make him simply amazing.

At the same time, Charlie disclosed that he never found a way to solve a complex problem, but he trains himself hard how to avoid them. He believes in a thinking game; at first, what he does is try to simplify the problem. Once he arrives at a conclusion or an opinion, he may have no longer have doubts and discussions with himself. He does not have some kind of ego, pretending that he is able to change people's minds and opinions if the facts are changing. He is not super protective and trying to confirm his opinion, relying only on confirmation bias.

He is aware of bad influences and controls his habits on everyday matters, such as avoiding people with bad reputations, alcohol, tobacco, and gambling. He is certain to follow the pattern of Benjamin Franklin.

Benjamin Franklin: "My intention being to acquire the habitude of all these virtues, I judged it would be well not to distract my attention by attempting the whole at once, but to fix it on one at the time; and, when I should be master of that, then to proceed to another, and so on, till I should have thro' the thirteen[cxliv]."

**Good Habits Are Beneficial. Bad Habits Have to Be Avoided**

Charlie: "The engineering idea of breakpoints that's a very powerful model. The notion of a critical mass that comes out of physics is a very powerful model. Tipping point is a very correct idea even at an individual level it's called habit. When Marley's miserable ghost says, 'I wear the chains I forged in life,' he is talking about chains of habit that were too light to be felt before they became too strong to be broken. The rare life that is wisely lived has in it many good habits cultivated and maintained and many bad habits avoided or cured[cxlv]."

Even Buffett has said that Charlie influenced him enormously.

Buffett: "If you've attended our annual meetings, you know Charlie has a wide-ranging brilliance, a prodigious memory, and some firm opinions. I'm not exactly wishy-washy myself, and we sometimes don't agree. In fifty-six years, however, we've never had an argument. When we differ, Charlie usually ends the conversation by saying: 'Warren, think it over and you'll agree with me because you're smart and I'm right.'"

"What most of you do not know about Charlie is that architecture is among his passions. Though he began his career as a practicing lawyer (with his time billed at fifteen dollars per hour), Charlie made his first real money in his thirties by designing and building five apartment projects near Los Angeles. Concurrently, he designed the house that he lives in today—some fifty-five years later. In recent years, Charlie has designed large dorm complexes at Stanford and the University of Michigan, and today, at 91 age, he is working on another major project[cxlvi]".

## Buffett: Berkshire Has Built to Charlie's Blueprint; My Role Has Been That of General Contractor

Warren Buffett: "From my perspective, though, Charlie's most important architectural feat was the design of today's Berkshire. The blueprint he gave me was simple: Forget what you know about buying fair businesses at wonderful prices; instead, buy wonderful businesses at fair prices. Altering my behavior is not an easy task (ask my family). I had enjoyed reasonable success without Charlie's input, so why should I listen to a lawyer who had never spent a day in business school (when—ahem—I had attended three). But Charlie never tired of repeating his maxims about business and investing to me, and his logic was irrefutable. Consequently, Berkshire has been built to Charlie's blueprint. My role has been that of a general contractor, with the CEOs of Berkshire's subsidiaries doing the real work as subcontractors[cxlvii]."

At Daily Journal's annual meeting in 2014, Charlie was asked, What daily habits would you recommend practicing?

Charlie: "I have never succeeded very much in anything in which I was not very interested. If you can't somehow find yourself very interested in something, I don't think you'll succeed very much, even if you're fairly smart. I think that having this deep interest in something is part of the game. If your only interest is Chinese calligraphy, I think that's what you're going to have to do. I don't see how you can succeed in astrophysics if you're only interested in calligraphy."

"The rare life that is wisely lived has in it many good habits cultivated and maintained and many bad habits avoided or cured. And the great rule that helps here is again from Franklin's *Poor Richard's Almanack*: 'An ounce of prevention is worth a pound of cure.' What Franklin is here indicating, in part, is that Inconsistency-Avoidance Tendency makes it much easier to prevent a habit than to change it[cxlviii]."

But what is the real impact all of these human characteristics have on Berkshire Hathaway? Berkshire Hathaway is the biggest decentralized company in the world. Everything about its operation is a colossal independent intelligent management. Warren Buffett and Charlie Munger's creation could be one of the biggest and most admirable business organizations in the world. Reliable people and trusted management, great businesses united together. The company no longer depends on unpredictable economic forces, even during recession times.

Adapting a policy of never depending on the mercy of a stranger, Berkshire is ready for new acquisitions, the policy avoided complicated decisions and businesses that bring unwanted controversy. He is very careful with the reputation of Berkshire saying, "If you lose money for the firm and I will be understanding. If you lose reputation I will be ruthless. Reputation is the most valuable gift you ever had[cxlix]."

Many of Buffett's critics accuse him of dividing his private and business life into two separate sets of moral books. I don't want to focus myself on issues of how their human qualities impact corporate structure. They both have the right ethical standard. As Charlie put it, "If you mix raisins with turds, they stay raisins and turds[cl]." So no tricks with the shareholders, give honest answers to all of their questions, hire great managers and people to this partnership, and avoid debts and standard calamities while treating shareholders fairly.

## Benjamin Franklin: I Am Not Moral Because It Is the Right Thing to Do but Because It Is the Best Policy

Charlie: "Ben Franklin said: 'I'm not moral because it's the right thing to do—but because it's the best policy.' We knew early how advantageous it would be to get a reputation for doing the right thing and it's worked out well for us. My friend Peter Kaufman, said, 'If the rascals really knew how well honor worked, they would come to it.' People make contracts with Berkshire all the time because they trust us to behave well where we have the power and they don't. There is an old expression on this subject, which is really an expression on moral theory: 'How nice it is to have a tyrant's strength and how wrong it is to use it like a tyrant.' It's such a simple idea, but it's a correct idea[cli]."

Charlie understands well the power of behavior; the unethical behavior could spread very quickly and destroy or even pollinate. "Avoid dealing with people of questionable character," and, "You can't form a business partnership with your frivolous, drunken brother in-law[clii]." Berkshire is an unusually rational place. It has a long perspective. There are no talks outside of the company to push it in a certain direction.

So, no external factors are pressing to deal with or pressing Warren Buffett and Charlie Munger on any decisions. That is a great way to operate, so as not to be misled by external factors, such as Wall Street's culture; there is no room for any stupidity and rapid decisions. To be independent thinkers is their choice, to avoid any pressures from other people and management.

Warren: "Like in internet stocks and neighbors having success and they have high IQs. It works for a while, that is a great danger period. It starts as skepticism, but neighbors get richer. We don't have any pressures to do that sort of thing. We don't think we are smarter than others; we just won't do stuff we don't understand. And we won't be jealous when others do well. That is what it is all about."

Charlie: "I always say there is a reason why this stuff is in the Bible. Can't covet your neighbor's ass. They were having trouble with envy a long time ago. It is the one sin there is no fun."

Buffett: "This group of companies sells products ranging from lollipops to jet airplanes. Some of the businesses enjoy terrific economics, measured by earnings some unleveraged net tangible assets that run from 25 percent after tax to more than 100 percent.

"A few, however, have very poor returns, a result of some serious mistakes I made in my job of capital allocation. These errors came about because I misjudged either the competitive strength of the business being purchased or the future economics of the industry in which it operated. I try to look out ten or twenty years when making an acquisition, but sometimes my eyesight has been poor. Charlie's has been better; he voted no more than 'present' on several of my errant purchases[cliii]."

Both Charlie and Warren have an extensive intelligence network of people and companies they have access to, practically to every company in the United States.

### Charlie: When You Don't Know and You Don't Have Any Special Competence, Don't Be Afraid to Say So

Charlie: "When you don't know and you don't have any special competence, don't be afraid to say so."

Reporter: "You discussed Coke's mistake. Do you have any thoughts about where Apple went wrong?"

Charlie: "Let me give you a very good answer—one I'm copying from Jack Welch, the CEO of General Electric. He has a Ph.D. in engineering. He's a star businessman. He's a marvelous guy. And recently, in Warren's presence, someone asked him, 'Jack, what did Apple do wrong?' His answer? 'I don't have any special competence that would enable me to answer that question.' And I'll give you the very same answer. That's not a field in which I'm capable of giving you any special insight. On the other hand, in copying Jack Welch, I am trying to teach you something. When you don't know and you don't have any special competence, don't be afraid to say so. There's another type of person I compare to an example from biology. When a bee finds nectar, it comes back and does a little dance that tells the rest of the hive, as a matter of genetic programming, which direction to go and how far. So about forty or fifty years ago, some clever scientist stuck the nectar straight up. Well, the nectar's never straight up in the ordinary life of a bee. The nectar's out. So the bee finds the nectar and returns to the hive. But it doesn't have the genetic programming to do a dance that says straight up. So what does it do?

"Well, if it were like Jack Welch, it would just sit there. But what it actually does is to dance this incoherent dance that gums things up. And a lot of people are like that bee. They attempt to answer a question like that. And that is a huge mistake. Nobody expects you to know everything about everything. I try to get rid of people who always confidently answer questions about which they don't have any real knowledge. To me, they're like the bee dancing its incoherent dance. They're just screwing up the hive[cliv]."

This is why I am writing this book with extreme curiosity and interest. Why don't more value investors follow this path of morality? These rules and principles of course belong to the leaders in value investing, but mostly they are human characteristics. Most investors today are antagonistic, have bad ethics and behavior, act stupidly and have no discipline, make everyday trading, and try to be the first to predict the market—this Wall Street culture with its greed, speculation, and hate. Buffett and Munger are deeply hated by Wall Street investors for their success and discipline.

Buffett: "Charlie and I don't expect to win many of you over to our way of thinking—we've observed enough human behavior to know the futility of that—but we do want you to be aware of our personal calculus. And here a confession is in order: in my early days I, too, rejoiced when the market rose. Then I read chapter eight of Ben Graham's *The Intelligent Investor*, the chapter dealing with how investors should view fluctuations in stock prices. Immediately the scales fell from my eyes, and low prices became my friend. Picking up that book was one of the luckiest moments in my life[clv]."

### Bob Rodriguez: The Best Advice I Ever Got from Charlie

I would also like to focus your attention on the interview piece "Bob Rodriguez: The Best Advice I Ever Got" which was published in *Fortune*:

"In the fall of 1974 I was in graduate school at USC taking a portfolio-management investment course. The financial markets were in difficulty, and I didn't understand how securities were being sold at such depressed levels. I had only recently discovered Security Analysis by Graham and Dodd when we had a guest lecturer come in named Charlie Munger, who went on about this idea of value investing. After the class was over, I walked up to Charlie and asked him if there was one thing that I could do that would make me a better investment professional. His answer was, 'Read history, read history, read history.' And so, I became a good historian, reading both economic and financial history as well as general history.

"What I learned is that people relate to the crises they have experienced. So when the crisis of 2008 came, it felt like an old friend to me because it had so many similarities to the banking crisis of 1907. Asking Charlie's advice and then reading history allowed me to put those things in context[clvi]."

Actually being a billionaire and one of the richest people in America presumes certain responsibilities in the area of philanthropy. Charlie chose to focus on education. It is an area where he has a good understanding. Charlie has years of experience at Caltech, at Michigan University, at Harvard. He understands how these organizations and institutions work. What are typical problems or certain areas where his money could really benefit? I don't think Charlie sees charity work lightly. I suppose he might think it a mistake to contribute to charity without his philosophy behind it. Charity should be governed by the same principals as business or in education.

## Charlie Is Giving Back

Charlie: "Those of us who have been very fortunate have a duty to give back[clvii]." Charlie has long been involved in philanthropy. Among his charities are Good Samaritan Hospital, Planned Parenthood, Stanford University Law School, Harvard Westlake School, University of Michigan, Stanford University, Polytechnic School in Pasadena, and Los Angeles YMCA.

"Although Mr. Munger left the University of Michigan before graduating, he became one of its most generous donors when he pledged $110 million in 2014 for graduate student housing and fellowships[clviii]."

In 2014 Charlie directed $100 million of his gift to build a housing complex where graduate students from varying disciplines can live together and avoid the social isolation that so often accompanies graduate study. The remaining $10 million went toward a graduate fellowship program designed to encourage study and interaction among graduate students in different fields.

He gave these gifts because he believes housing has a big effect on one's education.

Charlie "It's very uncommon that administrations are much interested in creating dormitories because if you're an elite place and you've got ten applicants for every spot, it's perfectly natural to think, 'Why the hell do we need to do any more for the students? They're begging to get in,'" he says. "I don't think you abuse your best customers merely because you can get by with it[clix]."

This isn't his first donation of this sort. In 2011 he gave $20 million to the university's law school to renovate housing for law students. He decided to donate the money now rather than give it as a bequest so he can see the results of his giving.

Charlie: "I'm soon going to be departed from all of my money," he said. "Why not give more of it away while I get the fun of giving it[clix]?"

Two other organizations benefited from Mr. Munger's gifts in 2013. He donated $32 million to the Huntington Library, Art Collections and Botanical Gardens in Los Angeles for a new education and visitor center that is scheduled to open in 2015. His wife, Nancy, was a Huntington trustee; not including this most recent gift, Mr. Munger has donated about $27 million to the organization over almost three decades. In addition, he gave nearly $1.9 million to the Marlborough School, a private girls' school in Los Angeles, for an athletics center. His wife was an alumna of the school, as were a daughter, two granddaughters, and a daughter-in-law[clxi].

Charlie Munger governs his philanthropy as he and Buffett run Berkshire's business model. This severed him and Berkshire great during all of these years, so why treat philanthropy different. As a big believer in education and study, I am not very surprised by his choice; are you?

Charlie always knew that he needed this more efficient way of disposing of his fortune. It was at the same time clear for him that without a consolidated principle and strategy, this large amount of his money would just get wasted. As Charlie has repeated many times,

## Do Not Have a Master Plan

Charlie commented at the Wesco 2004 annual meeting: "And there has never been a master plan. Anyone who wanted to do it, we fired because it takes on a life of its own and doesn't cover new reality. We want people taking into account new information[clxii]."

This is a correct statement. Berkshire has been governed under the cult pressure of Buffett and Munger when the right opportunities arise. But back to my favorite part of this research, which is about human habits and the cultivation of principles of honesty, morality, and rationality, which bring Charlie so far ahead of the pack. And as a human he is very careful when it comes to certain habits and principles. Who could do it different? Charlie just hates people who are lazy and unreliable; he just cannot stand fools.

Warren Buffett: "John mentioned Ben Graham, who was my teacher at Columbia University. When he was twelve years old, he sat down and made a list of the qualities he admired in other people, and he made a list of the qualities he found unattractive in other people. He decided that it was just an act of will and tan habit to develop those attractive qualities and get rid of the unattractive qualities. Anybody can show up on time, they cannot claim credit for ideas that are not their own, they cannot cut corners, they can avoid envy. All these things are doable and they make an enormous difference in how you function, not only in your job but in society subsequently. I'll give you more illustration. Let's just assume when you got out of school, that you won a lottery of some sort and you were enlisted to pick any of your classmates, and you got 10 percent of his earnings for the rest of his or her life. You had about an hour to make up your mind. Now we'll leave out picking the son or daughter of the richest person around or something of the sort; let's say we're all starting from scratch. Now, who would you pick? Just think about that for a moment. You wouldn't give them an IQ test. You probably wouldn't look at their grades. You'd probably think, who's going to function best, when they get out there? If they had a 300-horsepower motor, who's going to get 300 horsepower out of it instead of 150 or 100? You'd look for who is going to function best. And, you would look for people with those qualities that you admire, but which are also attainable by you and which become a matter of habit after time.

"Somebody said that, the chains of habit are too light to be felt until they're too heavy to be broken. It is absolutely true that the habits of behavior you start out with will follow you the rest of your life. And as you think about that person whom you would like to buy the 10 percent of, the person whom you find admirable or attractive, the answer is that if you want to sit down and do it yourself, you can be the one that you would buy 10 percent of. It is not that difficult. One friend of mine said that in hiring they look for three things, intelligence, energy, and character. If they can't have the last one, the first two will kill you because it's true, if you are going to hire somebody that doesn't have character, you really better hope they are dumb and lazy, because, if they are smart and energetic, they'll get you in all kinds of trouble. Well that's enough of the advice[clxiii]."

## Warren Buffett and Charlie Munger Correlation

Thomas Jefferson said: "In matters of style, swim with the current. In matters of principle, stand like a rock[clxiv]."

Through this honesty and support with decisions and problems, Munger helped Buffett enormously. Charlie's contribution was his traditional emotionalism as one of the most important criteria for being a successful investor. Contrarianism in managing money is a basic requirement for success in investing. The contrarianism combined with knowledge, wisdom, integrity, and Charlie is priceless for Buffett.

One more attribute of Charlie described by Buffett: "If you've attended our annual meetings, you know Charlie has a wide-ranging brilliance, a prodigious memory, and some firm opinions. I'm not exactly wishy-washy myself, and we sometimes don't agree. In fifty-six years, however, we've never had an argument[clxv]".

But how hard is it to get rid of your own bad habits later on?

Buffett: "Among your friends, there is one person you most want to emulate and who you would want to be least like. You can approach this by thinking about which of your peers you would want to own 10 percent of for the rest of their lives and which ones you would like to short. Then identify the qualities that make you want to emulate them and try to internalize those qualities. Do the opposite for the friends you would want to short. You are currently still young and can get rid of your bad habits[clxvi]".

Both Munger and Buffett believe you could not do it automatically, to learn how to develop these habits; it is up to you to follow these role models.

Charlie: "Another idea that I got, and this may remind you of Confucius too, is that wisdom acquisition is a moral duty; it's not something you do just to advance in life. Wisdom acquisition is a moral duty. As a corollary to that proposition which is very important. It means that you're hooked for a lifetime of learning, and without lifetime learning you people are not going to do very well. You are not going to get very far in life based on what you already know. You're going to advance in life by what you're going to learn after you leave here."

## Learn the Method of Learning

As Charlie loves to put it from Alfred North Whitehead: "Just as civilization can progress only when it invents the method of invention, you can progress only when you learn the method of learning." Charlie is very reserved, amazingly patient, but at the same time, he never tries to persuade some people to behave a certain way.

There is another story from *Outstanding Investor Digest* on this issue.

Reporter: "At the end of your article in *Outstanding Investor Digest*, you mentioned that only a select few investment managers actually add value. Since you're speaking to an audience of future lawyers, what do you encourage us to do in order to be able to add value in our profession?"

### Get Your Moral Code Straight

Charlie: "To the extent you become a person who thinks correctly, you can add great value. To the extent that you have learned it so well that you have enough confidence to intervene where it takes a little courage, you can add great value. And to the extent that you can prevent or stop some asininity, which would otherwise destroy your firm, your client or something or someone that you care about, you can add great value.

"And there are constructive tricks you can use. For example, one reason my old classmate, Joe Flom of Skadden Arps, had been such a success-ful lawyer is that he is very good at dreaming up little, vivid examples that serve to pound the point home in a way that really works. It is enormously helpful when you are serving clients or otherwise trying to persuade some-one in a good cause to come up with a little humorous example. The ability to do that is a knack. So you could argue that the Joe Floms of the world are almost born with a gift. But he has honed the gift. And to one degree or another, all of you were born with this gift. And you can hone it, too.

"Occasionally, you get into borderline stuff. For instance, suppose you have got a client who really wants to commit tax fraud. If he doesn't push the tax law way beyond the line, he can't stand it. He can't shave in the morning if he thinks there's been any cheating he could get by with that he hasn't done. And there are people like that. They just feel they are not living aggressively enough.

"You can approach that situation in either of two ways: (A) you can say, 'I just won't work for him', and duck it. Or, (B) you can say, 'Well, the circumstances of my life require that I work for him.' And what I'm doing for him doesn't involve me cheating. Therefore, I'll do it. And if you see he wants to do something really stupid, it probably won't work to tell him, 'What you are doing is bad. I have better morals than you.' That offends him. You're young. He's old. Therefore, instead of being persuaded, he is more likely to react with, 'Who in the hell are you to establish the moral code of the whole world?'"

As we know, being a Warren partner, Charlie chose to cultivate a wise approach; he saw himself as a silent partner. Practicing contrarianism, as not so many investors are following these principles, I would like to turn your attention to only some of them who I believe follow Warren Buffett and Howard Marks. Howard Marks is famous value investor[clxvii].

In one of his interviews, Howard Marks has very good examples of what it means to be a contrarian.

Howard Marks: "How do you avoid getting trapped by the devil? I've been in this business for over forty-five years now, so I've had a lot of experience. In addition, I am not a very emotional person. In fact, almost all the great investors I know are unemotional. If you're emotional, then you'll buy at the top when everybody is euphoric then prices are high. Also, you'll sell at the bottom when everybody is depressed and prices are low. You'll be like everybody else and you will always do the wrong thing at the extremes.

"Therefore, unemotionalism is one of the most important criteria for being a successful investor. And if you can't be unemotional, you should not invest your own money, period. Most great investors practice something called contrarianism. It consists of doing the right thing at the extremes, which is the contrary of what everybody else is doing. So unemtionalism is one of the basic requirements for contrarianism[clxviii]."

As a Russian classical writer, Fyodor Dostoevsky, wrote: "If not reason, then the devil[clxix]."

Let us move on what Buffett thinks about contrarian ideas and his definition of it:

"Warren Buffett, how do you develop a conviction for contrarian ideas? How do you perceive the risk?"

Buffett: "At Berkshire we have certain filters that have been developed. If the course of a presentation or the evaluation part of a proposal or if an idea hits a filter then there is no way I will invest. Charlie has similar filters. We don't worry about a lot of things as we only have to be right about a certain number of things—things that are within our circle of competence. A great example is the Nebraska Furniture Mart. Mrs. B took cash because she didn't understand stocks. It is important to know what I can do. I have no idea which company will dominate in the auto industry in the next five years so I don't pick. I prefer simple things in my circle of competence. Good decisions scream at you. For example, in 2008 you shouldn't have been afraid just because assets were cheap. In your entire investment lifetime, you may have six times when this happens and it is 'raining gold[clxx].'"

## Avoid Deadly Sins. Start with the Right Morality First

Charlie: "When I read my psychology talks given about fifteen years ago, I realized that I could now create a more logical, but much longer 'talk,' including most of what I had earlier said. Despite four very considerable objections, I decided to publish the much-expanded version. Why am I doing this? My third and final reason is the strongest; I have fallen in love with my way of laying out psychology because it has been so useful for me[clxxi]".

Envy is one of the Catholic Church seven deadly sins. In the Book of Genesis[2], Cain kills his brother Abel out of envy because God prefers his sacrifice.

Charlie said, "The idea of caring that someone is making more money faster than you is one of a deadly sins. Envy is really stupid sin because it is the only one you could never possible have any fun at[clxxii]".

---

[2] https://en.wikipedia.org/wiki/Book_of_Genesis

## Learning to Change Your Previous Conclusions Is a Key

He seemed to have a tremendous faith in himself to prove that study and the search for wisdom could be fun. Enjoying his lifestyle, collecting mental models all-around of many disciplines, Charlie likes to play bridge. A self-taught person, he collects and has cultivated a taste for books. He is not focused on certain decisions or standards of thinking. He has repeated many times "both Warren and I are very good at changing our prior conclusions. We work at developing that facility because without it, disaster often comes." This creation of culture for reality recognition is a characteristic of Charlie, but you have to remain very strange to understand that, to change your point of view on any issues, and to confirm that your previous conclusions were incorrect. As opposed to denying the new facts and information, he tries to be objective as much as he can.

Charlie understands that a lot of faults and mistakes are coming from psychology. Charlie: "When people get bad news, they hate the messenger." Faults and massive mistakes happen if people ignore the psychology. At the same time, Charlie likes some rules being called "no-fault rules[clxxiii]."

Charlie: "I like the Navy system. If you're a captain in the Navy, and you've up for twenty-four hours straight and have to go to sleep, and you turn the ship over to a competent first mate in tough conditions, and he takes the ship aground—clearly through no fault of yours—they don't court martial you, but your naval career is over.

"You can say, 'That's too tough. That is not law school. That's not due process.' Well, the navy model is better in its context than would be the law school model. The navy model really forces people to pay attention when conditions are tough—because they know that there is no excuse.

"It does not matter why your ship goes aground. Nobody is interested in your fault. It is just a rule that we happen to have—for the good of all, all effects considered. I like some rules like that. I think that the civilization works better with some of these no-fault rules. But that stuff tends to be anathema around law schools. 'It's not due process. You're not really searching for justice.' Well, I am searching for justice when I argue for the Navy rule—for the justice of fewer ships going aground. Considering the net benefit, I don't care if one captain has some unfairness in his life. After all, it is not like he is being court marshaled. He just has to look for a new line of work. And he keeps vested pension rights and so on. So it is not like it is the end of the world. So I like things like that. However, I'm in a minority[clxxiv]."

Rational Charlie is self-minded; he is usually sizing up the world skeptically. He is a tall man; Charlie could speak hours long on his favorite subjects. Both an energetic and very silent partner, he is very colorful both in his action as a silent advisory to Buffett and in his speech, with a clear way of thinking. He has an unusual way of behaving compared with money managers on Wall Street: no emails and phone calls, no special wishes in organizing meetings, and no obsession for beating the market. Quietly sitting in his room reading and thinking is his way of life. By organizing his life to tune out distractions and make fewer decisions, Charlie is focused on making more quality decisions and avoiding rapid solutions on everything. How could it be different? Ruling with principle first while being able to play tomorrow? Berkshire Hathaway has cash reserves that could have been spent during the bottom of a panic market.

Charlie Munger, being a vice chairman of Berkshire Hathaway, runs a company called the Daily Journal Corporation (DJCO). This California publisher more than tripled its value since the financial crisis of 2008. Charlie is well known for his colorful and very controversial comments, not just on Buffett and Berkshire, but also on the world's mistakes in both economic and financial matters.

I like that definition of Berkshire Charlie answered to Ms. Loomis from Ms. Loomis of *Fortune* asked a question on behalf of a shareholder in the audience: "How would you explain Berkshire and its value premise to the investor's thirteen-year-old daughter?"

Mr. Munger took his first crack: "We like to stay sane while others go crazy. That is competitive advantage." He also noted that the company tries to be a good steward to its subsidiaries and a good partner.

"This was a very good idea," he said drolly. "I wish we'd done it on purpose[clxxv]."

Charlie combined the right ethics and morals with intelligence and great intellect. Charlie was definitely born skeptical, so it's no wonder he sees the world through his own prism, with all of the mistakes and frauds, but at the same time he likes to be surrounded with people and friends who are sincere to him and others.

Knowing the most typical important mistakes and misjudgments in life and value investing, he immediately understands what a person has to say about him, if one is jealous or envious. Mostly people just want to know how to become rich and how to make it very fast without time and persistence.

Reporter: "What do you think is the least talked about or most misunderstood moat around the business?"

Mr. Munger: "Everybody would really like to have a misunderstood moat. You're the greediest fellow that's spoken. All you want to know is if I have a moat that you can understand that other people don't. Have a modest wish. You are going to ask an ninety-one-year old man how to do it? Reminds me of one of my favorite stories. A young man comes to Mozart and says, 'With your help I want to compose symphonies.' He says, 'Look, you were doing symphonies when you were ten years of age. I'm twenty-one.' Mozart says, 'Yes, but I wasn't running around asking other people how to do it[clxxvi].'" This is very Charlie.

### Do Not Multitask. You Waste Your Time

One of my favorite quotes of Charlie is from a Daily Journal meeting. He was asked: "How did you balance reading that much and having so many children?" He answered, "When I want to read something, I take everything else down. I don't know a wise person who doesn't read a lot."

"I think that people who multitask pay a huge price: they can't think of anything deeply, giving the world an advantage, which they shouldn't give. I wouldn't succeed doing it. I did not succeed in life by intelligence. I succeeded because I have a long attention span[clxxvii]."

I believe Charlie grew more comfortable after years of working with Buffett, and he developed a powerful loyalty to him. Both men struggle to reduce the number of mistakes they make.

Charlie from a Daily Journal Meeting in 2016: "Warren and I and JP Guerin do two things. One, we spend a lot of time thinking. Our schedules are not crowded, and we look like academics more than businessmen. It is a soft life waiting for a few opportunities, and we seize them and are ok with waiting for a while and nothing happens. Warren is sitting on an empire, and all he has on his schedule is a haircut this week. He has plenty of time to think. Luckily, so many of you groupies are so obscure, you'll have plenty of time to think. Second, multitasking is not the highest quality thought man is capable of doing unless you're chief nurse of hospital. If not, be satisfied with life in shallows. I didn't have a number two plan; I wasn't going to dance lead in Bolshoi Ballet or stand on the mound in Yankee Stadium. The constant search for wisdom or opportunity is important. It applies to the personal life too. [clxxviii]."

### Marrying the Best Person Who Wants You Is the Most Important Decision You Can Make

Charlie: "Most of you aren't going to have five or six opportunities to marry a wonderful person. Most of you aren't going to get one. Most of you get an ordinary chance, which leads to an ordinary result[clxxix]."

But if you see Charlie—patient, kind, and silent from the first—you will realize later that his humor is full of small stories of human behavior, of mistakes and humorous anecdotes. He has an ability to be silent and is reluctant to argue directly.

One example from Warren Buffett: "It reminds me that whenever I get a little worried about Charlie, maybe I shouldn't talk about it. There is a joke about not hearing well that goes like this. I have this wonderful partner, but I think his hearing is going. What should I do? The doctor told me to stand across room. So I stood across room and said, 'I think we ought to buy GM at thirty-five.' No response. I go halfway across the room, say it again, and no response. So I walk right over to him and say, 'Charlie I think we ought to buy GM at thirty-five.' AND he says, for the third time, YES! So speak up.[clxxx]"

Charlie has talent for influencing Buffett in almost all decisions of capital allocations at Berkshire. United by the same values, Buffett and Munger have made Berkshire a very unusually rational place. They are not in a hurry and have no shareholders outside pushing them in different directions. It is a great way to operate, ignoring the stupidity and opinions of Wall Street. So once again, no external factors are influencing these great minds.

A born contrarian, Charlie insisted upon buying in declining markets and selling in rising ones. He never provided any direct market advice, what to buy and what to sell. Buffett, as one may notice, very rarely makes decisions on any subject without previous consultations with his "silent partner." He just needs that cooperation. By creating a new form of partnership, which has grown into a corporation, Buffett has been able to fuse together different industries and firms to a seamless whole.

Warren Buffett must be accepted as the greatest business mind that America ever produced.

Charlie has a different character from Warren Buffett; if you watch BRK's annual meetings, Charlie is usually carefully listening to each question and Buffett answers. Charlie does not say a single word. He never misses a point. He has an ability to concentrate on specific issues and matters and thinks it through before answering. This is a unique characteristic of Charlie Munger. He would go away from a person he is speaking with without saying a word, not even goodbye. By concentrating on a problem or question for the next day, Charlie will announce his position, working out the answer after careful consideration.

Charlie handled his money very well. His courage combined with patience applied in the most difficult of times. Sticking to his purpose and unshakable confidence make him simply an amazing human being. We do not often see Charlie react emotionally. He seems to possess a strong power of confidence. He usually sees a little further than everybody else. It is very hard to surprise him with any question. He has mastered a method of solving matters, giving himself time to think and then time to act. At the same time, if he has made up his mind on a certain issue, he is still able to change. Any decision at any time could be stopped, recalled, and changed.

Charlie Munger, ninety-one years old in 2015, is ranked on *Forbes*' revered list of the world's billionaires at number 465 in the United States and number 1,415 globally. Journalists, investors, money managers, as envious critics, assail him and Warren Buffett. Wherever Charlie goes, be it Berkshire's annual meeting or a DJCO (Daily Journal Corporation) meeting, he is surrounded by an army of groupies, the people who like him so much, and his fans. Charlie sometimes jokes about it.

Charlie: "Many of you people are here because you're investment groupies, not Daily Journal shareholders[clxxxi]."

At the same time, being famous may create pressure to give back to society. As opposed to Warren Buffett, Charlie does not like too much attention from the public. For someone of Munger's private nature, it is not that pleasant to be surrounded by press and fans all the time. Charlie wants privacy for his studies, his private life.

Charlie said after being listed on the *Forbes* billionaire's list, "I'm somewhat ashamed...That I've profited from being shrewd with money is not itself satisfying to me. To atone, I teach and try to set an example. I would hate it if the example of my life caused people to pursue the passive ownership of pieces of paper. I think lives so spent are disastrous lives. I think it's a better career if you help build something. I wish I'd built more, but I was cursed at being so good at stock picking. 'The man is the prisoner of his talents.' You can laugh, but I'll bet this room is full of people who are prisoners of their talents. It tends to be the human condition[clxxxii]."

Personal charity is not an area that Charlie ever wants to delegate to someone else; he gets a certain pleasure from doing this work himself. Charlie: "I try to make up for it with philanthropy and meetings like this one today. This meeting is not out of kindness. This is atonement[clxxxiii]."

## Back to Benjamin Franklin

You hear all the time that we look for practical people. These are money managers, intellectuals, and politicians—generally, all those sorts of people could be found in any quantity you like—but there are less practical people with brains and morality. Nowadays, there is no doubt a complete lack of people, lack of personal initiative among young people. Maybe the reason to blame is that there is a lack of heroes. Charlie Munger found his hero at a very young age; his main hero is Benjamin Franklin. He has tried to emulate Franklin's ideas throughout his life. Franklin has a lot to teach us about money and behavior, ethics and morals.

Franklin said: "If everyone is thinking alike, then no one is thinking[clxxxiv]." Charlie just loves Franklin, who avoided a crowd opinion. He is obsessed with Franklin's wisdom and has adopted his hero's call for a multidisciplinary education. Charlie already understood early in life that to be smart, one must have models in his head. One of two models just aren't enough. "To the man with only a hammer, every problem looks like a nail. So, it is a perfectly disastrous way to think and perfectly disastrous way to operate in the world[clxxxv]."

**Don't We Pay a Very High Price for Not Learning from Our Heroes?**
Benjamin Franklin: "When I was a child of seven years old, my friends on a holiday filled my pocket with coppers. I went directly to a shop where they sold toys for children; and being charmed with the sound of a whistle, that I met by the way in the hands of another boy, I voluntarily offered and gave all my money for one. I then came home, and went whistling all over the house, much pleased with my whistle, but disturbing the entire family. My brothers, sisters, and cousins, understanding the bargain I had made, told me I had given four times as much for it as it was worth, put me in mind what good things I might have bought with the rest of the money, and laughed at me so much for my folly, that I cried with vexation; and the reflection gave me more chagrin than the whistle gave me a pleasure. This, however, was afterward of use to me, the impression continuing on my mind; so that often, when I was tempted to buy some unnecessary thing, I said to myself Don't give too much for the whistle gave me a pleasure.

"As I grew up, came into the world, and observed the action of men, I thought I met with many, very many, who gave too much for the whistle. When I saw one too ambitious of court favor, sacrificing his time in attendance on levees, his repose, his liberty, his virtue, and perhaps his friends, to attain it, I have said to myself, this man gives too much for his whistle. When I saw, another tend of popularity, constantly employing himself in political bustles, neglecting his own affairs, and ruining them by that neglect. He pays, indeed, said I, too much for your whistle. If I knew a miser, who gave up every kind of comfortable living, all the pleasure of doing good to others, all the esteem of his fellow citizens and joys of benevolent friendship, for the sake of accumulating wealth, Poor man, said I, you pay too much for our whistle. When I met with a man of pleasure sacrificing every laudable improvement of the mind, or of his fortune, to mere corporeal sensations and ruining his health in their pursuit, mistaken man, said I, you are providing pain for yourself, instead of pleasure, you give to a man for your whistle. If I see one fond of appearance, or fine clothes, fine houses, fine furniture, fine equipages, all above his fortune, for which he contracts debts, and ends his career in a prison, Alas, say I, he has paid dear, very dear, for his whistle. When I see a beautiful sweet-tempered girl married to an ill-natured brute of a husband, what a pity, say I that she should pay so much for a whistle! In short, I conceive the great part of the miseries of mankind are bought upon them by false estimates they have made of the value of things and by their giving too much for their whistles[clxxxvi]."

Charlie Munger about Franklin: "There is the sheer amount of Franklin's wisdom. And the talent. Franklin played four instruments. He was the nation's leading scientist and inventor, plus a leading author, statesman, and philanthropist. There has never been anyone in our lifetime like him…Franklin was quite old when he was ambassador to France. This was after he was world famous and rich, and he was more self-indulgent than when he was young and making his way in the world. But he was a very good ambassador, and whatever was wrong with him from John Adams's point of view helped him with the French. I think Franklin was a marvelous steward. I'm willing to take the fellow as he averaged out. And certainly, I'm in favor of old people having a little enjoyment[clxxxvii]."

In business, Charlie would like to ensure from the beginning before making any decision that he knows the rules. Like in bridge, he is not playing to be beaten. He is disciplined and has a prepared mind in every detail in order to beat the odds. When he has a plan for action, he brings in easy and quick decisions. The problem or issue could look complicated, but not for Charlie, who already thought it through and takes it directly to the point. He devotes a tremendous amount of his time to books to have a right-thinking tool to apply to any problem or complex situation. One may say that Charlie was trained from the beginning to work, to be disciplined, and to save the money. As Benjamin Franklin said, "A penny saved is a penny earned." Buffett himself agrees that Berkshire Hathaway was shaped tremendously by the way Charlie approached practice and discipline. It of course has a big impact on Warren Buffett as well. As from his childhood, Charlie early took the path to be an adult and growing as an adult. He has an exaggerated sense of responsibility in everything he does; he took that habit with him throughout his life.

"Benjamin Franklin! Remember that time is a money!clxxxviii".

## Avoid Sloth and Unreliability

Charlie: "What do you want to avoid? Some answers are easy. For example*sloth and unreliability will fail. If you are unreliable, it does not matter what your virtues are, you're going to crater immediately. So, faithfully doing what you're engaged to do should be an automatic part of your conduct. Of course, you should avoid sloth and unreliability." Charlie idolized his main hero Benjamin Franklin. From the books, including biographies, on Charlie, we could not confirm any evidence that Charlie was ever influenced by gossip, or people's opinion. He maintains mostly indifference to crowd opinion. He trained himself to be like that.

### Humble Charlie Munger

Charlie once described himself: "Most people who try will end up unpopular and unsuccessful. There are certain peculiarities of my personality that I would not recommend. My irreverence. My insistence. These things will get most people into trouble…Basic morality works for everyone. Discipline works for everyone. Objectivity works for everyone. That's what you should focus on[clxxxix]."

His comments and answers are more constructive rather than critical. He answered some question about his family's investment participation of BRK; he persisted that they stay with Berkshire no matter what happen, being confident, that it could outperform the S&P Index.

The newspapers were all the time puffing and questioning Warren Buffet about being one of the America richest men and about his major philanthropic bequest and future planning.

However, not so many questions are for Charlie as he has no pressure or large responsibility as Buffett. Charlie have chosen his favorite charities a long time ago. Education was a neutral and safe area for philanthropy for him. No less than in business, Charlie prefers to monitor the philanthropic activities himself. Through this strategy, it strengthens a young generation to be better prepared in life, better educated to survive or even to win the evolution struggle. He finds it dangerous just to throw money at people who are in need,.

It seemed at first that the mutual interest in psychology and business might be a bridge between Buffett and Munger. Deep insight into psychology happened to be very useful for Charlie.

Charlie: "When I read my psychology talks given about fifteen years ago, I realized that I could now create a more logical but longer 'talk,' including most of what I have earlier said. Despite four very considerable objections, I decided to publish the much-expanded version. Why I am doing this…My third and final reason is the strongest: I have fallen in love with my way of laying out psychology because it has been so useful for me."

As he aged, Charlie had the same way of humble living as his hero, Benjamin Franklin. Charlie likes to welcome his friends and visitors. Not so often, he agrees to interviews. Charlie indulges his two consuming hobbies: playing bridge and I believe still reading. Surrounded by friends and family, being not extensively engaged in Berkshire on a daily basis, Charlie lives more freely than before. Charlie's brilliant intelligence and capacity as a businessman likely could be researched through his comments and speeches. He has shown the value of his expert opinion as a businessmen in both for-profit and nonprofit work.

# Chapter Three

## Charlie Munger and Lee Kuan Yew

One of Charlie Munger's heroes is Lee Kuan Yew. In a *Forbes* interview on May 22, 2010, Charlie said, "If I were Lee Kuan Yew (formidable former Singapore leader), I'd make finance less attractive to go into[cxc]."

Charlie: "We would do better coping with complex systems if we thought about them more. Lee Kuan Yew thinks things through. The fact that it is unpleasant does not stop him. Affluence and poverty can both ruin children. Charlie recommends a much more rational and tough-minded approach. An ounce of prevention is not worth a pound; it is often worth ten[cxci]."

Charlie: "Is there an example of a prudent decision like the Marshall Plan after World War II? The George Washington of Singapore, Lee Kuan Yew, decided to marry the smartest girl in his class. Their son is now the PM of Singapore. He was very practical man. He didn't want people dying of malaria, so he drained all the swamps and didn't care if a little fish went extinct. He didn't like the drug problem and he looked around the world to solve the drug problem. He found the solution in the US by copying the US military's policy. Any time you can be tested, and if you fail, you go to jail. If something was going to grow like a cancer, he would check it hard with the wrath of God. He turned a country with no resources or agriculture into a prosperous country starting from zero miles per hour. We need to pay more attention in our country to the Singapore model. They hate Lee Kuan Yew in liberal arts colleges. They hate that Singapore does not allow free speech. But time after time he has been successful, and even the leaders in China came to Singapore and learned from Lee Kuan Yew[cxcii]."

Charlie does not care whether the cat is black or white, as long as it catches mice. In many respects, the United States is too damn permissive.

Charlie "We do not step hard enough on things that can grow into trouble. If some of the silly accounting practices had been stopped, then none of this would have happened[cxciii]." In a Q&A at the University of Michigan in 2010, Charlie Munger praised Lee Kuan Yew and the Singapore model in response to a question posted by a student: "If you could design a system, how would you take into consideration so that it enables rationality[cxciv]?" Besides praising Singapore's system of eradicating the drug problem, smoothing out racial tensions, and making the island "user-friendly," Munger praised Lee Kuan Yew for thwarting the Asian trend of marrying a good-looking wife with big breasts to going for someone smarter than he was.

Charlie: "If you will make a study of the life and work of Lee Kuan Yew, you will find one of the most interesting and instructive political stories written in the history of mankind. This is better than Athens…and you will learn a lot that will be useful in your whole life.

"Study the life and work of Lee Kuan Yew; you're going to be flabbergasted[cxcv]."

Charlie Munger 2015 Daily Journal Meeting:

Q: "Charlie, I'm here from Sydney, Australia. I'd like to just come back to Lee Kuan Yew. What are the chances of that culture continuing with the current government and future governments of Singapore?"

Mr. Munger: "They're pretty good. Lee Kuan Yew left a base, eliminated the corruption, made it hard to get in, and paid the people a lot. There is no real incentive to steal in Singapore. Either in Parliament or as an advanced government administrator, you get paid very well, and you're admired, and so forth. I think what he has left Singapore will continue to do very well. But of course, he rose when he was doing it, and China wasn't. Now Singapore has to compete with China. China makes it harder."

Reporter: "What about the changes since his son or predecessor came in, for example, allowing casinos to come to Singapore?"

Mr. Munger: "I would have hated that. You make so much money running a casino, compared to any normal human business. There are no inventories; it's like having a license to print money, and people just can't stand temptation. So, he organized a casino business. Only foreigners can play; he didn't want to ruin the locals. I would not have slept with the devil that much. But Yew was no longer really in power when that happened. If he'd still been young, I'd like to think he would not have done that[cxcvi]."

Charlie Munger at Berkshire Hathaway's annual meeting in 2007:

"The work has been heavily concentrated in one mind, Warren Buffett. Sure, others have had input, but Berkshire enormously reflects the contributions of one great simple mind. This is not how we normally live in democracy; everyone takes turns. But if you really want a lot of wisdom, it's better to concentrate decisions and process in one person. It's no accident that Singapore has a much better record, given where it started, than the United States. There, power was concentrated in one enormously talented person, Lee Kuan Yew, who was the Warren Buffett of Singapore[cxcvii]."

Wikipedia: "Lee Kuan Yew, known to be the man who transformed Singapore from a poor society into one of Asia's wealthiest nations, Lee Kuan Yew is often called a 'benevolent dictator.' As a leader who was in power for thirty-one years from 1959 until 1990, he implemented some laws that were deemed autocratic, and often opted to dismantle political opposition. Despite this, he is often looked upon favorably for his transformation of Singapore, and is considered by many to be one of the most successful political pragmatists[cxcviii]."

The importance of prevention resonates with Lee Kuan Yew and Charlie Munger as a main principle. Many smart people understand the role and importance of prevention. Mostly mistakes would have been better fixed before they ever arose. Excellent books on human behavior and mistakes from incentives have been written by Robert Cialdini,

Richard Thaler and Daniel Kahneman. So such bad habits as a lack of patience, of discipline, and of concentration have a strong tendency to repeat themselves.

Lee Kuan Yew: "All great religions, all great movements, all great political ideologies start off saying 'let's make human being as equal as possible.' In fact, he is not equal—never will be." Lee Kuan Yew, in his interview during Shell's 120th anniversary in 2013, was asked, "What is the meaning of life?" And he answered the following: "Life is what you make of it. You're dealt a pack of cards. Your DNA is fixed by your mother and your father... Your job is to do the best of the cards that have been handed out to you. What can you do well? What can you not do well? What are you worst at? If you ask me to make my living as an artist, I'll starve. Because I can't draw. But if you ask me to do mathematical questions or to argue and point out, I'll get by. Those are the cards I handed out—and I make use of them[cxcix]."

Do not try to do something you were not favored by nature to do. You have noticed that Charlie Munger and Warren Buffett are the big believers in the circle of competence. Each of us has to find out what he or she is doing the best in life and then just concentrate on this area.

Charlie: "I wasn't going to dance lead in Bolshoi Ballet[cc]." Play your hand to the best of your skills, abilities, and talents. Staying inside of your own circle of competence is crucially important. As Warren Buffett told you, you have to know where the borders are.

### Lee Kuan Yew: I Am Not Depressed; I Am Realistic

Reporter: "Finland has produced Nokia and Sweden IKEA...These are companies that seem to punch way above what the country's physical size seem to suggest...

Lee Kuan Yew: All right, Sweden, IKEA....do we want to go into (retail and furniture)—have we got the wood and designers? The Swedes are good designers. Nokia was one of these flukes in history, from an economist—a controlled society, overshadowed by the Soviet Union, they broke through. But they are about what, 7 to 8 million? Can they keep up the competition from Korea? From Japan? Watch it in the long term. How many bright fellows have you got? With inventive and creative minds?

Female reporter: "You are making us all very depressed."

Lee Kuan Yew: "No. I am not depressed—I am realistic. I say these are our capabilities; this is the competition we face, and given what we have—our assets and capabilities—we can still make a good living, provided that we are realistic[cci]."

The same ideas and principles govern private life. So, the importance of genes and being rational in choosing a partner. Lee Kuan Yew did not believe in love at first sight.

## Lee Kuan Yew: I Don't Believe in Love at First Sight. I Think It Is Grave Mistake

Lee Kuan Yew: "I don't believe in love at first sight. I think it's a grave mistake. You're attracted by physical characteristics, and you will regret it[ccii]." But one shouldn't think Lee Kuan Yew was emotionless and a poor, unhappy man. He definitely wasn't. He was married to his wife Kwo Geok Cheo for sixty years. She helped him to govern Singapore. In his biography, *The Singapore Story*[cciii], Lee Kuan Yew writes that he was confident Kwo Geok Cheo could be a sole breadwinner and bring up the children, therefore giving him an "insurance policy" so that he could enter politics, unimpeded by financial concerns or parental responsibilities. Lee Kuan Yew picked Kwo Geok Cheo as his partner not just based on physical attraction, but based on her intelligence and apparent genetic potential.

Lee Kuan Yew: "There are many sons of doctors who have married doctors. Those who married spouses who are not as bright are tearing their hair out because their children can't make it. I have lived long enough to see all this play out.

"So when the graduate man does not want to marry a graduate woman, I tell him he's a fool, stupid. You marry a non-graduate, you're going to have problems, some children bright, some not bright. You'll be tearing your hair out[cciv]."

About Lee Kuan Yew, Charlie said at the University of Michigan in 2010, "Time after time after time he's done his thing. His approach to marriage was interesting. The average very successful man in the Asian culture. There is exceptionally good-looking women though somewhat dumber than he is. This is the system. Well, this guy Lee Kuan Yew was so smart that he was the second-ranked school student in his high school. The student who was one-tenth of a percentage point higher was female. So, he didn't follow the Asian rule of marrying the beautiful women with the big boobs—the little darling that you are. He married this woman who was a tenth of a point higher. Who is now the prime minister of Singapore? Their son. This is a very unusually successful man and a very unusually successful history[ccv]." Both Lee Kuan Yew and Charlie

Munger avoided popularity, as they had their own mission. Lee Kuan Yew: "I have never been over concerned or obsessed with opinion polls or popularity polls. I think a leader who is, is a weak leader[ccvi]." Charlie Munger explained how Lee Kuan Yew made Singapore such an attractive country to invest in. "He figured out what he wanted to attract, then he made the situation very user friendly for those people[ccvii]."

Who were "those people"? They were wealthy investors, world leaders, and others who just wanted stability. A few examples of Lee Kuan Yew's achievements. Drug dealing is punishable by death. Chewing gum has been banned. Littering is fined with thousands of dollars, and if you do it three times, you are forced to wear a badge that says "I am a little boy." Problems were solved in a crafty way: for example, malaria was a big problem. Lee Kuan Yew found the root of the problem, a nearby swamp. He drained the entire swamps, without regard for the protest of some squeamish environmentalists. "Who cares if some strange fish species goes extinct? Human lives are at stake[ccviii]."

Charlie: "If you want to study, you take Singapore. Terrible malaria problem, it's a swamp. Drains all swamps. Who's going to care if some little fish dies? He's got a drug problem. He searches the world over for the right solution to drug problem. He finds it in the US. Isn't that a very interesting thing? Somebody in Singapore reading books and deciding United States was the answer to Singapore problems. He copied the military's drug policy. Anybody in Singapore would pee in a bottle instantly on demand and if they flunked, would immediately go on a tough compulsory rehab. Away went the drug problem. Just time after time after time he made these winning decisions. He wanted the place to be prosperous. He wanted best people to come in, and he made the civilization very user friendly to who he wanted to attract. And it worked[ccix]!"

### Charlie Munger was gifted with an advantageous DNA

Ideas make all the difference in life; copy, copy, and copy wise men and great ideas. In this book, I want to convince you that there is no success story based on personal qualities and abilities as an individual. These ideas are not coming from nothing. Most of the ideas could be studied and acquired by you for further implementation in business and life. At the beginning, one may think that Charlie Munger is a genius by himself, but this is not the case; however, he was gifted with an advantageous DNA, which includes the love for learning and reading. The information and knowledge he acquires through his studies give him extraordinary opportunities to bet on stocks more successfully, work harder, see more advantages for capital allocation, which the rest of the world does not see. From his childhood Charlie, like most people, was suffering and struggling in life to achieve success. He was not born with a superhuman brain but acquired the knowledge for superior decision-making.

It would be easier to accept the version that Charlie just met Warren Buffett at an event and that alone is the explanation behind the success of Berkshire Hathaway. But it is not that simple. The combination of Charlie's ambitions, abilities, opportunity, and intellectual advantage are strong contributing factors. If you ask, "Does Charlie have a special talent?" the answer is "Yes," but his talent is a combination of different skills. His biggest talent, I still believe, is everyday preparation. In his early teenage years, Charlie was reading a lot of widely different literature—psychology, philosophy, mathematics, and theoretical physics. He was blessed to be born into a family where the value of education was the first priority. Charlie has a lot of friends and admirers, but he is definitely lonely, which is evident from his special talents to think independently, ignoring the opinion of others. The persistence and determination were obviously already a part of his character at birth. Charlie trained, as one may see, to always look at a problem trying to identify the logic and system, whereas others would take on an emotional approach. Despite being a lonely character, he still possesses excellent social skills and is always surrounded by friends and family. Charlie portrays a strong feeling of stoicism and is able to stand up after the worsts falls in life.

Charlie: "At a certain point, you gotta say to people, 'Suck it in and cope, buddy. Suck it in and cope.' And in the '30s with my family, these families would move into the same house, and they wore the same clothes for a while. They coped. And that was part of how civilization got through. We do not want a civilization where every hardship we go to the government and say, 'Give me some money. The world is not what I expected.' So, I think there's too much danger in just shoveling out money too much to people who say, 'My life is a little harder than it used to be.' Of course, it's a little harder than it used to be! That is normal worldly life[ccx]."

Charlie has this willingness to question authority, a quality that makes many people almost dislike him, but the same quality has turned out to be the biggest treasure in the constant search for wisdom and learning through reading. The ability to challenge the conventional wisdom is therefore not the worst human quality to have.

With so many qualities and talents, Charlie chose to be the silent partner of Warren Buffett. You may ask why. But Charlie definitely enjoys his position. He rationalized that he has less talent for other subjects. His impudence and contempt for convention mean that he has no qualms about challenging the power of academic education, criticizing the lack of multidisciplinary education.

Challenging controversial wisdom as the truth for everybody was so obvious but Charlie never accepted it without skepticism. The ability to think the problem through and to concentrate helped him a lot in eliminating the irrelevant faults from the main issue or problem.

Probably, if Charlie took a job as university professor or any academic job, his originality in thinking and criticism would not be the best qualities for succeeding. He would definitely face pressure to confront to the prejudices.

Charlie has a unique aristocracy of intellect. A strength of Charlie Munger's mind is that it can juggle a variety of concepts and ideas at the same time. Education and wisdom seeking bring him satisfaction and joy. One of his strengths as an independent thinker is the ability to eliminate distractions, to be able to fully concentrate and work, completely ignoring the opinions of others—his immortal power of concentration.

The value of a collage education, as Charlie has pointed out, is not in learning facts and disciplines, but training the mind to enhance its thinking abilities. He strongly believes that morality has to rise above the "individual wishes." You should live your life according to moral codes that will benefit humanity. Consider the fact that Charlie, as an excellent thinker, can change his attitudes when confronted with new evidence.

# Final Thoughts

I would like for more schools and educational institutions to adapt and teach something similar to the latticework approach by Charlie, because only this path is a correct way to becoming wise. Of course, we do have Farnam Street Blog and other sources, which you can find on the internet, but unfortunately, this information is not available in a consolidated format. I would love to see people cultivating these models and supporting each other to implement them into practice, so they would bring more people working and studying together. I do believe Charlie's ideas are studied in elite schools and universities, and they will influence the world. We all need a tool kit of mental models for better thinking. They will help determinate the right path, and the people who want to swim better than others will follow them. We do need a tool kit to make advanced decisions; we need to draw on different attributes and abilities, to solve any problems. Culture matters.

*But if you are a gambler, no matter what you think, you are on the wrong path. Get out of it quickly.* If you are losing, you are wrong, but you are wrong also if you win. Compulsive gambling is an illness to which man could lose nearly everything man loves.

The most useful mental models from Charlie's tool kit are basic mathematics, compound interest, and elementary psychology. If you do not do it, you are giving a huge advantage to everybody else. What Charlie found interesting is that our brain will not immediately follow this track.

Charlie: "If you don't get this elementary, but mildly unnatural, mathematics of elementary probability into your repertoire, then you go through a long life like a one-legged man in an ass-kicking contest. You are giving a huge advantage to everybody else. One of the advantages of a fellow like Buffett, whom I've worked with all these years, is that he automatically thinks in terms of decision trees and the elementary math of permutations and combinations.

"So you have to learn in a very usable way this very elementary math and use it routinely in life—just the way if you want to become a golfer, you can't use the natural swing that broad evolution gave you. You have to learn to have a certain grip and swing in a different way to realize your full potential as a golfer."

I do believe there is a huge interest of the public to study Munger's mental models. It is a great pleasure to tell you my story of Charlie Munger to be a unique human and exceptional thinker. As we do know from Charlie Munger's *Almanack* book, through the Great Depression, struggling as a family, the Mungers supported each other through the hard times. Charlie started to work very young in order to earn money and assist his parents and as soon as possible to be a breadwinner. Charlie was aware of his uncle, who was an architect struggling in the unemployed market. It was his first serious lesson on how to survive and adapt to the lessons of life. I think some lessons of human lack of rationality, mistakes, and faults were burned into his head. From early age, he developed a strong desire to be an independent thinker and not depend on anyone else. He wanted to be a real man, to be useful and work hard.

I think from his childhood, Charlie knew that a multidisciplinary approach to self-learning would bring him into the better position. I think Charlie Munger from an early age was behaving as an adult with good judgment and not like a boy of his age who really enjoyed his childhood.

We do not know if the Mungers had servants and helpers when Charlie was a small boy. His father, mother, and grandfather started to be his role models. Well, in our days everybody wants to be rich young and thinks that poverty should be abolished. Mostly people take many things for granted—great books, newspapers, paper, pens, and pencils. When Charlie started to work for Warren Buffett's grandfather, he got just six dollars per week for this job.

Charlie, with his independence from circumstances and people, started to think relatively early about how money could make more money without him paying attention. It is very similar to Warren Buffett's approach to money.

Later in life Charlie, being a lawyer, was not happy to serve and to work for other people with problems. He did not like to run around the people to satisfy them, and to be paid for it. He always wanted to have the independence of capitalist.

My question to you right now is this: Do you think that being poor and struggling helps poor boys to be better survivors later on in life, once they have survived conflicts, wars, great depression, and major family issues?

I think the answer is yes, they do possess advantages. Watch the life itself to learn it the hard way. Without being spoiled with expensive things and wealth, they can just learn and understand life better. Self-learning and discipline work. These boys later in life always march straight to the front and lead the world as Charlie Munger has done. They are disciplined and possess a competitive advantage among others. They are advanced in the human race. It is much like Confucianism: simple, they are not ashamed of who they are. They are dedicated to education, plan their life with integrity and honesty, and set an example for the next generation, to encourage others to behave well in life.

Will it promote prosperity? I think so. Upon the speculation of our technological future, we do want to know future technology predictions and scenarios, but it seems unwise for me to predict it. However, our duty is to emulate the best people such as Charlie Munger and his best ideas. Mostly people forget that when bad times come, people with morality and integrity fear less than others. These are obviously simple rules, but the young generation of the race, in order to get an independent existence and wealth, have to be ethical learning machines. God bless Charlie Munger and his family.

## Author Biography

Oxana Dubrovina is inspired by Charlie Munger and his guiding principles to life, business and value investing. She has used these guidelines in her own life as a business and corporate lawyer.

Ms. Dubrovina received law degrees from the University of Moscow and the University of Vienna. She spent ten years working in international law in Vienna before moving to the United States. Now Oxana lives in Houston, Texas, with her husband and two children. In her spare time, she enjoys keeping up with the latest business news, reading international literature, and immersing herself in foreign languages. She speaks Russian, English, German, and Norwegian. She has also cultivated a deep love of Mandarin after her time living in Shanghai, China.

Oxana Dubrovina is the creator of the Charlie Munger Almanack Group on Facebook. She invites you to join her there at www.facebook.com/groups/754138784714366.

# The Art of Being Rational: Charlie Munger

## A NOTE OF SORCES

Hundreds of studies have been on conducted over years on successes and mistakes in business at Berkshire Hathaway. It could easily double the pages of this book if we will try to put cognitive mistake and behavior human errors. I have focused on my portrait of Charlie Munger, so his most important quotes, comments his recommendations for further reading and behavior. The knowledge in this book is based on my research last five years.

[i] Charlie Munger, CNBC interview, Sunday, May 6, 2012

[ii] Influence The Psychologie of Persuasion by Robert Cialdini. New York Harper Collins, 1993

[iii] Charlie Munger CNBC interview, 6.06.2012

[iv] Charlies T.Munger, Poor Charlies Almanack, extended third version. Virginia Beach The Donning Company Publishers, 2006

[v] The Darwin Reader, page, 28. Edited by Morton Bates and Philips Homphery, London 1957

[vi] Warren Buffett Letter to Shareholders of Berkshire Hathaway, 2013.

[vii] Warren Buffett Letter to Shareholders of Berkshire Hathaway, 2015.

[viii] *Behind the Scenes* with Berkshire Hathaway Billionaire Charlie Munger by Janet Lowe on 30.10.2000 JOHN WILEY & SONS, INC. New York

[ix] Charlies T.Munger, Poor Charlies Almanack, extended third version. Virginia Beach The Donning Company Publishers, 2006

[x] Daily Journal Corporation 2013, Notes of Whitney Tilson

[xi] 1994, Warren Buffett Lecture at the University of Nebraska

[xii] Charlie Munger, 2011 Berkshire Hathaway Meeting.

xiii Painting. The Body of Dead Christ in the Tomb by Hans Holbein Kunstmuseum Basle made in 1521

xiv Michael D.Eisner. Why Great Partnership Succeed Working Together. 2010

xv The *Psychology of Human Misjudgment*, a *speech* given in *1995* by *Charlie Munger, Harvard University*

xvi Thoughts to build on by M. R. Kopmeyer Published 1970 in <u>Louisville.</u>

xvii *USC Law Commencement Speech | Charlie Munger. University of South California* May 13,2007

xviii *WESCO Financials, Notes of Whitney Tilson 2006*

xix *Charlie Munger* University of *Michigan Ross* School *2017*

xx Charlies T.Munger, Poor Charlies Almanack, extended third version. Virginia Beach The Donning Company Publishers, 2006

xxi Daily Journal Corporation 2017, Notes of Whitney Tilson

xxii Warren Buffett Letter to Shareholders of Berkshire Hathaway, 2003

xxiii Warren Buffett Letter to Shareholders of Berkshire Hathaway, 2017

xxiv A Conversation with Charlie Munger 2008 DuBridge lecture at Caltech

xxv A Conversation with Charlie Munger 2008 DuBridge lecture at Caltech

xxvi *Munger*: *A Lesson* on *Elementary*, *Worldly Wisdom As It Relates To Investment Management & Business*. February 20, 2012

xxvii *The Art of Stock Picking*, Charlies T.Munger, Poor Charlies Almanack, extended third version. Virginia Beach The Donning Company Publishers, 2006

xxviii The *Psychology of Human Misjudgment*, a *speech* given in *1995*, *Charlie Munger, Harvard University*

xxix *USC Law Commencement Speech | Charlie Munger. University of South California* May 13, *2007*

xxx *USC Law Commencement Speech | Charlie Munger. University of South California* May 13, *2007*

xxxi The *Psychology of Human Misjudgment*, a *speech* given in *1995* by legendary investor *Charlie Munger, Harvard University*

xxxii The *Psychology of Human Misjudgment*, a *speech* given in *1995* by legendary investor *Charlie Munger, Harvard University*

xxxiii The *Psychology of Human Misjudgment*, a *speech* given in *1995* by legendary investor *Charlie Munger, Harvard University*

xxxiv *Charlie Munger USC Business School* in *1994*, A *Lesson on Elementary Worldly Wisdom*

xxxv Charlies T.Munger, Poor Charlies Almanack, extended third version. Virginia Beach The Donning Company Publishers, 2006

xxxvi *Securities Trading Investigation*. WARREN BUFFETT, CHAIRMAN, *SALOMON BROTHERS* SEPTEMBER 4, *1991* https://www.c-span.org/video/?21029-1/securities-trading-investigation

xxxvii Q&A: *Legal Matters with Charles* T. *Munger. May 15, 2009* https://law.stanford.edu/stanford-lawyer/articles/qa-legal-matters-with-charles-t-munger/

xxxviii Daily Journal Corporation 2013, Notes of Whitney Tilson.

xxxix Warren Buffett. Lecture at the *University of Nebraska*. 1991 Notes of Whitney Tilson

xl The *Psychology of Human Misjudgment*, a *speech* given in *1995* by *Charlie Munger, Harvard University*

xli *USC Law Commencement Speech | Charlie Munger. University of South California* May 13, *2007*

xlii *USC Law Commencement Speech | Charlie Munger. University of South California* May 13, *2007*

xliii *USC Law Commencement Speech | Charlie Munger. University of South California* May 13, *2007*

xliv Warren and Charlie and the chocolate factory. http://fortune.com/2012/08/22/warren-and-charlie-and-the-chocolate-factory/

xlv Charlie Munger speech at UC Santa Barbara 2003: "*Academic. Economics: Strengths* and Faults *After Considering. Interdisciplinary Needs*"

xlvi *USC Law Commencement Speech | Charlie Munger. University of South California* May 13, *2007*

xlvii *Charles Munger: A Lesson on Elementary, Worldly Wisdom*. Harvard *Business School, USC Business School, 1994*

xlviii *WESCO Financials, Notes of Whitney Tilson 2004*

xlix *USC Law Commencement Speech | Charlie Munger. University of South California* May 13, *2007*

l *USC Law Commencement Speech | Charlie Munger. University of South California* May 13, *2007* li *Charles Munger*: *A Lesson on Elementary*, *Worldly Wisdom*. revisted *1997*

lii Charlies T.Munger, Poor Charlies Almanack, extended third version. Virginia Beach The Donning Company Publishers, 2006.

liii Charlies T.Munger, Poor Charlies Almanack, extended third version. Virginia Beach The Donning Company Publishers, 2006.

liv A Fireside Chat With Charlie Munger Sep 12, 2014 https://blogs.wsj.com/moneybeat/2014/09/12/a-fireside-chat-with-charlie-munger/

lv A Fireside Chat With Charlie Munger Sep 12, 2014 https://blogs.wsj.com/moneybeat/2014/09/12/a-fireside-chat-with-charlie-munger/

lvi The *Psychology of Human Misjudgment*, a *speech* given in *1995* by *Charlie Munger, Harvard University*

lvii *USC Law Commencement Speech | Charlie Munger*. *University of South California* May 13, *2007*

lviii *Charlie Munger 1986 Harvard Commencement speech*

lix *Charlie Munger 'Academic Economics: Strengths and Weaknesses, after Considering Interdisciplinary Needs,' at the University of California at Santa Barbara, 2003.*

lx Charlie Munger at. Harvard-Westlake School. January 19, 2010. http://csinvesting.org/wp-content/uploads/2014/07/Munger-Talk-at-Harvard-Westlake.pdf

lxi *Charlie Munger* at *Harvard-Westlake School*. January *19, 2010* http://csinvesting.org/wp-content/uploads/2014/07/Munger-Talk-at-Harvard-Westlake.pdf

lxii Daily Journal Corporation 2014, Notes of Whitney Tilson

lxiii The *Psychology of Human Misjudgment*, a *speech* given in *1995* by legendary investor *Charlie Munger, Harvard University*

lxiv *Charlie Munger 'Academic Economics: Strengths and Weaknesses, after Considering Interdisciplinary Needs,' at the University of California at Santa Barbara, 2003.*

lxv *Charlie Munger*. "*A Lesson on Elementary*, *Worldly Wisdom* As It Relates to Investment Management & Business." At Harvard *Business School*, *USC Business School*, 1994

lxvi Charlies T.Munger, Poor Charlies Almanack, extended third version. Virginia Beach The Donning Company Publishers, 2006

lxvii *'Academic Economics: Strengths and Weaknesses, after Considering Interdisciplinary Needs,' at the University of California at Santa Barbara, 2003.*

lxviii *'Academic Economics: Strengths and Weaknesses, after Considering Interdisciplinary Needs,' at the University of California at Santa Barbara, 2003.*

[lxix] *WESCO Financials, Notes of Whitney Tilson 2007*

[lxx] *WESCO Financials, Notes of Whitney Tilson 2006*

[lxxi] *WESCO Financials, Notes of Whitney Tilson 2005*

[lxxii] *Charles Munger: A Lesson on Elementary, Worldly Wisdom* As It Relates To Investment Management & Business. Harvard *Business School 1996*

[lxxiii] Daily Journal Corporation 2015, Notes of Whitney Tilson

[lxxiv] *Charlie Munger 'Academic Economics: Strengths and Weaknesses, after Considering Interdisciplinary Needs,' at the University of California at Santa Barbara, 2003*

[lxxv]

[lxxvi] *The Autobiography of Benjamin Franklin* written by *Benjamin Franklin*

[lxxvii] Charlie Munger - Caltech 2008 DuBridge Distinguished Lecture in Beckman Auditorium

[lxxviii] *God's Utility Function. Extracts* from *Scientific American*, p.80-85, November *1995* article by *Richard Dawkins* adapted from a chapter of "River Out of Eden: A Darwinian View* of *Life" Basic Books, 1995* http://www.physics.ucla.edu/~chester/CES/may98/dawkins.html

[lxxix] *Speech* of *Charles* T. *Munger, Investment Practices of Leading Charitable Foundations* October *14, 1998*

[lxxx] *If—"* is a poem by English Nobel laureate *Rudyard Kipling*, written circa 1910

[lxxxi] *Speech* by *Charlie Munger* to the *Harvard* School. JUNE 13, *1986*

[lxxxii] *USC Law Commencement Speech | Charlie Munger. University of South California* May 13, *2007*

[lxxxiii] The *Psychology of Human Misjudgment*, a *speech* given in *1995* by legendary investor *Charlie Munger, Harvard University*

[lxxxiv] The *Psychology of Human Misjudgment*, a *speech* given in *1995* by legendary investor *Charlie Munger, Harvard University*

[lxxxv] The *Psychology of Human Misjudgment*, a *speech* given in *1995* by legendary investor *Charlie Munger, Harvard University*

[lxxxvi] The *Psychology of Human Misjudgment*, a *speech* given in *1995* by legendary investor *Charlie Munger, Harvard University*

[lxxxvii] The *Psychology of Human Misjudgment*, a *speech* given in *1995* by legendary investor *Charlie Munger, Harvard University*

[lxxxviii] The *Psychology of Human Misjudgment*, a *speech* given in *1995* by legendary investor *Charlie Munger, Harvard University*

[lxxxix] The *Psychology of Human Misjudgment*, a *speech* given in *1995* by legendary investor *Charlie Munger, Harvard University*

[xc] Daily Journal Corporation 2014, Notes of Whitney Tilson.

[xci] Charlie Munger at Harvard-Westlake School January 19, 2010

[xcii] Charlie Munger at Harvard-Westlake School January 19, 2010

[xciii] 11/10/00 TALK OF CHARLES T. MUNGER TO BREAKFAST MEETING OF THE PHILANTHROPY ROUND TABLE.

[xciv] Man's Search for Meaning is a 1946 book by Viktor Frankl

[xcv] *USC Law Commencement Speech | Charlie Munger. University of South California* May 13, *2007*

[xcvi] *USC Law Commencement Speech | Charlie Munger. University of South California* May 13, *2007*

[xcvii] Damn Right!: Behind the Scenes with Berkshire Hathaway Billionaire Charlie Munger: Janet Lowe.

[xcviii] http://joekusnan.tumblr.com/post/7113195673/charlie-mungers-last-meeting

[xcix] *USC Law Commencement Speech | Charlie Munger. University of South California* May 13, *2007*

[c] *USC Law Commencement Speech | Charlie Munger. University of South California* May 13, *2007*

[ci] Warren Buffett speech given at Harvard in 1998

[cii] Berkshire's Charlie Munger Speaks. CNBC 1:36 PM ET Fri, 4 May 2012.

[ciii] Warren Buffett Speech University of Nebraska in 1994

[civ] Charlie Munger's famous talk at USC Business School in 1994 A Lesson on Elementary Worldly Wisdom

[cv] Wit and Wisdom from Poor Richard's Almanack (Dover Thrift Editions) Benjamin Franklin

[cvi] *USC Law Commencement Speech | Charlie Munger. University of South California* May 13, *2007*

[cvii] Damn Right!: Behind the Scenes with Berkshire Hathaway Billionaire Charlie Munger: Janet Lowe 2000

[cviii] Charlie Munger's famous talk at USC Business School in 1994 A Lesson on Elementary, Worldly Wisdom As It Relates to Investment Management & Business. From Poor Charlie's Almanack: The Wit and Wisdom of Charles T. Munger, Expanded Third Edition Publisher: Walsworth Publishing Company; 3rd edition (2005)

[cix] The *Psychology of Human Misjudgment*, a *speech* given in *1995* by legendary investor *Charlie Munger, Harvard University*

[cx] Proposals Relating to the Education of Youth in Pennsylvania 1749 by Benjamin Franklin

[cxi] Robert F. Sayre; Benjamin Franklin: His Life As He Wrote It. Ed. by Esmond Wright. (Cambridge: Harvard University Press, 1990

[cxii] Poor Charlie's Almanack: The Wit and Wisdom of Charles T. Munger, Expanded Third Edition Publisher: Walsworth Publishing Company; 3rd edition (2005)

[cxiii] The Harvard Classics - Autobiography of Benjamin Franklin, Journal of John Woolman, Fruits of Solitude book

[cxiv] *Charlie Munger 'Academic Economics: Strengths and Weaknesses, after Considering Interdisciplinary Needs,' at the University of California at Santa Barbara, 2003.*

[cxv] Poor Charlie's Almanack: The Wit and Wisdom of Charles T. Munger, Expanded Third Edition Publisher: Walsworth Publishing Company; 3rd edition (2005)

[cxvi] The *Psychology of Human Misjudgment*, a *speech* given in *1995* by legendary investor *Charlie Munger, Harvard University*

[cxvii] The *Psychology of Human Misjudgment*, a *speech* given in *1995* by legendary investor *Charlie Munger, Harvard University*

[cxviii] Charlie Munger's famous talk at USC Business School in 1994 A Lesson on Elementary, Worldly Wisdom As It Relates to Investment Management & Business. From Poor Charlie's Almanack: The Wit and Wisdom of Charles T. Munger, Expanded Third Edition Publisher: Walsworth Publishing Company; 3rd edition (2005)

[cxix] 2007 Law School Commencement address at the University of Southern California on May 13th

[cxx] 2007 Law School Commencement address at the University of Southern California on May 13th

[cxxi] Excerpt from Forbes Magazine. "The not-so-silent partner" by Robert Lenzner and David. S. Fondiller, January 22, 1996.

[cxxii] *WESCO Financials, Notes of Whitney Tilson 2005*

[cxxiii] *WESCO Financials, Notes of Whitney Tilson 2005*

[cxxiv] *WESCO Financials, Notes of Whitney Tilson 2005*

[cxxv] *WESCO Financials, Notes of Whitney Tilson 2005*

[cxxvi] *WESCO Financials, Notes of Whitney Tilson 2005*

[cxxvii] *USC Law Commencement Speech | Charlie Munger. University of South Califor-*

*nia* May 13, *2007*

cxxviii *USC Law Commencement Speech | Charlie Munger. University of South Califor-nia* May 13, *2007*

cxxix *WESCO Financials, Notes of Whitney Tilson 2005*

cxxx https://www.forbes.com/2010/05/12/charlie-munger-warren-buffett-markets-streettalk-berkshire-hathaway.html#4543a17e3833

cxxxi Charlie Munger's famous talk at USC Business School in 1994 A Lesson on Elementary, Worldly Wisdom As It Relates to Investment Management & Business. From Poor Charlie's Almanack: The Wit and Wisdom of Charles T. Munger, Expanded Third Edition Publisher: Walsworth Publishing Company; 3rd edition (2005)

cxxxii From Whitney Tilson's note from the 2007 Wesco Annual Meeting

cxxxiii *WESCO Financials, Notes of Whitney Tilson 2007*

cxxxiv Calvin Coolidge 30 President of US from Purpose and Persistence Are Required for Success: Unrewarded Genius Is Almost a Proverb Calvin Coolidge? Theodore Thornton Munger? M. M. Callen? Orison Swett Marden? Edward H. Hart? https://quoteinvestigator.com/2016/01/12/persist/

cxxxv *USC Law Commencement Speech | Charlie Munger. University of South Califor-nia* May 13, *2007*

cxxxvi *Charlie Munger 'Academic Economics: Strengths and Weaknesses, after Considering Interdisciplinary Needs,' at the University of California at Santa Barbara, 2003.*

cxxxvii Charlie Munger's famous talk at USC Business School in 1994 A Lesson on Elementary, Worldly Wisdom As It Relates to Investment Management & Business. From Poor Charlie's Almanack: The Wit and Wisdom of Charles T. Munger, Expanded Third Edition Publisher: Walsworth Publishing Company; 3rd edition (2005)

cxxxviii https://www.omaha.com/money/ex-billionaire-charlie-munger-on-recent-dona-tions-i-won-t/article_3f68516d-e2a6-58a9-ad24-0e117fb8e819.html Ex-billionaire Charlie Munger on recent donations: 'I won't need it where I'm going'

cxxxix Berkshire's 2008 annual meeting, Warren Buffett

cxl *USC Law Commencement Speech | Charlie Munger. University of South Califor-nia* May 13, *2007*

cxli Investors earn handsome paychecks by handling Buffett's business https://www.

omaha.com/money/investors-earn-handsome-paychecks-by-handling-buffett-s-business/article_bb1fc40f-e6f9-549d-be2f-be1ef4c0da03.html DJCO, *Notes of Whitney Tilson 2005*

cxliii Poor Charlie's Almanack: The Wit and Wisdom of Charles T. Munger, Expanded Third Edition Publisher: Walsworth Publishing Company; 3rd edition (2005)

cxliv Autobiography of Benjamin Franklin by Benjamin Franklin http://www.gutenberg.org/ebooks/20203

cxlv

cxlvi Warren Buffett Letter to Shareholders of Berkshire Hathaway, 2011

cxlvii Berkschire Hathaway Anual Meeting 2014

cxlviii Daily Journal Corporation annual meeting in 2014

cxlix https://finance.yahoo.com/news/moment-america-met-warren-buffett-115906138.html

cl From Poor Charlie's Almanack: The Wit and Wisdom of Charles T. Munger, Expanded Third Edition Publisher: Walsworth Publishing Company; 3rd edition (2005)

cli https://www.businessinsider.com/charlie-munger-on-the-wesco-merger-2011-7

clii https://www.businessinsider.com/warren-buffett-charlie-munger-quotes-at-berkshire-hathaway-annual-meeting-2015-5

cliii Berkshire Hathway Annural Report 2013

cliv http://static.fmgsuite.com/media/documents/62a7f3e8-62bc-4da2-87cb-dbd234d34667.pdf

clv Berkshire Hathaway Annual Report 2012

clvi http://archive.fortune.com/2012/02/07/news/companies/bob_rodriguez_best_advice.fortune/index.htm

clvii From Poor Charlie's Almanack: The Wit and Wisdom of Charles T. Munger, Expanded Third Edition Publisher: Walsworth Publishing Company; 3rd edition (2005)

clviii According to the chronicle of PHILANTHROPY www.philanthropy.com

clix https://www.philanthropy.com/article/Student-Housing-Receives/153619

clx https://www.philanthropy.com/article/No-17-Charles-Munger/153651

clxi https://philanthropynewsdigest.org/news/charles-munger-gives-32-million-to-huntington-library-for-education-center

clxii Wesco 2004 annual meeting

clxiii https://www.tilsonfunds.com/BuffettUofNebraskaspeech.pdf

clxiv Thomas Jefferson: The Art of Power - Kindle edition by Jon Meacham

clxv Berkshire Hathaway Annual Meeting 2014

clxvi https://grahamdoddsville.wordpress.com/2012/02/11/warren-buffett-talk-to-mba-students-from-the-university-of-georgia/

clxvii https://en.wikipedia.org/wiki/Howard_Marks_(investor)#cite_note-LAFund-21

clxviii https://advisoranalyst.com/glablog/2014/03/03/howard-marks-in-the-end-the-devil-always-wins.html/

clxix https://en.wikipedia.org/wiki/The_Brothers_Karamazov

clxx *Notes* from the *Meeting Dr*. *George* Athanassakos and *Ivey MBA and HBA students* had with Mr. *Warren Buffett*. Omaha, NB, February 27, *2015*. https://www.ivey.uwo.ca/cmsmedia/2953339/buffett-interview-2015.pdf

clxxi The *Psychology of Human Misjudgment*, a *speech* given in *1995* by legendary investor *Charlie Munger, Harvard University*

clxxii Poor Charlie's Almanack: The Wit and Wisdom of Charles T. Munger, Expanded Third Edition Publisher: Walsworth Publishing Company; 3rd edition (2005)

clxxiii Poor Charlie's Almanack: The Wit and Wisdom of Charles T. Munger, Expanded Third Edition Publisher: Walsworth Publishing Company; 3rd edition (2005)


clxxiv https://bambooinnovator.com/2013/07/24/charlie-munger-triples-publishers-value-with-panic-era-wager-on-stocks-unlike-munger-buffett-was-a-net-seller-of-stocks-at-berkshire-in-early-2009-as-the-company-faced-liabilities-on-deriv/

clxxv Warren Buffett Letter to Shareholders of Berkshire Hathaway, 2013

clxxvi Daily Journal Corporation Meeting 2015

clxxvii Daily Journal Corporation Meeting 2016

clxxviii Daily Journal Corporation Meeting 2016

clxxix Daily Journal Corporation Meeting 2016

clxxx Warren Buffett Letter to Shareholders of Berkshire Hathaway, 2014

clxxxi The Daily Journal (DJCO) 2013

clxxxii Notes from the 2001 Wesco Annual Meeting

clxxxiii Final Wesco Meeting: More from Charlie Munger

clxxxiv Autobiography of Benjamin Franklin by Benjamin Franklin http://www.gutenberg.org/ebooks/20203

clxxxv Charlie Munger's famous talk at USC Business School in 1994 A Lesson on Elementary, Worldly Wisdom As It Relates to Investment Management & Business. From Poor Charlie's Almanack: The Wit and Wisdom of Charles T. Munger, Expanded Third Edition Publisher: Walsworth Publishing Company; 3rd edition (2005)

clxxxvi Autobiography of Benjamin Franklin by Benjamin Franklin http://www.gutenberg.org/ebooks/20203

clxxxvii Charlie Munger's famous talk at USC Business School in 1994 A Lesson on Elementary, Worldly Wisdom As It Relates to Investment Management & Business. From Poor Charlie's Almanack: The Wit and Wisdom of Charles T. Munger, Expanded Third Edition Publisher: Walsworth Publishing Company; 3rd edition (2005)

clxxxviii https://founders.archives.gov/documents/Franklin/01-03-02-0130

clxxxix *Berkshire Hathaway Annual Meeting 2011*

cxc https://www.forbes.com/2010/05/12/charlie-munger-warren-buffett-markets-streettalk-berkshire-hathaway.html#7e38b2753833

cxci At Wesco Financial Corporation 2010

cxcii Charlie Munger speech University of Michigan 2010

cxciii Charlie Munger speech University of Michigan 2010

cxciv Charlie Munger speech University of Michigan 2010

cxcv Charlie Munger speech University of Michigan 2010

cxcvi Charlie Munger 2015 Daily Journal Meeting

cxcvii Charlie Munger at Berkshire Hathaway's annual meeting in 2007

cxcviii Wikipedia on Lee kuan Yew https://en.wikipedia.org/wiki/Lee_Kuan_Yew

cxcix *Lee Kuan Yew interview* during *2013* at *Shell's 120th anniversary, LKY* was asked "what is *the* meaning of life?" https://www.youtube.com/watch?v=_3PbIrtKndw

cc From Poor Charlie's Almanack: The Wit and Wisdom of Charles T. Munger, Expanded Third Edition Publisher: Walsworth Publishing Company; 3rd edition (2005)

cci *Hard Truths to Keep Singapore Going* Hardcover – 2011 by Lee Kuan Yew

ccii The Singapore Story: Memoirs of Lee Kuan Yew 1st Edition by Kuan Yew Lee Kuan Yew Lee Kuan Yew Lee (Author), Lee Kuan-Yeu (Author), Lee Kuan Yew (Author) 1999

cciii The Singapore Story: Memoirs of Lee Kuan Yew 1st Edition by Kuan Yew Lee Kuan Yew Lee Kuan Yew Lee (Author), Lee Kuan-Yeu (Author), Lee Kuan Yew (Author) 1999

[cciv] The Singapore Story: Memoirs of Lee Kuan Yew 1st Edition by Kuan Yew Lee Kuan Yew Lee Kuan Yew Lee (Author), Lee Kuan-Yeu (Author), Lee Kuan Yew (Author) 1999

[ccv] Charlie Munger speech University of Michigan 2010

[ccvi] *Lee Kuan Yew*: The *Grand Master's* In- sights on *China*, the *United States* and the. *World*. (Belfer Center Studies in International Security) Hardcover – February 1, 2013

[ccvii] Charlie Munger speech University of Michigan 2010

[ccviii] Charlie Munger speech University of Michigan 2010

[ccix] Charlie Munger speech University of Michigan 2010

[ccx] Charlie Munger speech University of Michigan 2010

Printed in Germany
by Amazon Distribution
GmbH, Leipzig

27925434R00127